Leaving Egypt

Leaving Egypt

*
Finding God
in the
Wilderness Places
*

Chuck DeGroat

SQUARE
INCH

Grand Rapids, Michigan

Leaving Egypt: Discovering God in the Wilderness Places. © 2011 Chuck DeGroat. Published by Square Inch, an imprint of Faith Alive Christian Resources, 2850 Kalamazoo Ave. SE, Grand Rapids, MI 49560. All rights reserved. With the exception of brief excerpts for review purposes, no part of this book may be reproduced in any manner whatsoever without written permission from the publisher. For information or questions about the use of copyrighted material in this resource please contact Permissions, Faith Alive Christian Resources, 2850 Kalamazoo Ave. SE, Grand Rapids, MI 49560; phone: 1-800-333-8300; fax: 616-726-1164; email:permissions@faithaliveresources.org.

Printed in the United States of America.

Cover image: iStock

We welcome your comments. Call us at 1-800-333-8300 or email us at editors@faithaliveresources.org.

Library of Congress Cataloging-in-Publication Data
DeGroat, Chuck.
Leaving Egypt: discovering God in the wilderness places / Chuck DeGroat.
    p. cm.
Includes bibliographical references (p. 308).
ISBN 978-1-59255-673-1 (alk. paper)
1. Christian life—Reformed authors. 2. Exodus, The—Typology. I. Title.
BV4501.3.D4457 2011
248.4—dc23

                                                                2011033349

10 9 8 7 6 5 4 3 2 1

Contents

Acknowledgments

Writing a book can teach you a lot about the Exodus journey. You're occasionally enslaved to little things like your laptop or big things like your reputation. You try your best to conquer the wilderness, only to find unexpected detours in your own writing and in your own heart. You battle inner voices of resistance ("You have nothing to say!") and face inevitable uncertainties ("Does it even matter?"). But if you're looking, you will recognize companions along the way. These have been my companions:

My wife, Sara, who loves me despite my own wilderness wanderings, and who brings my greatest joy in the journey.

My daughters, Emma and Maggie, who were sent directly from the promised land and bring laughter, happiness, and wilderness futility into my life.

An editor, Len VanderZee, who brings the precision of a scholar and the heart of a pastor.

And Jesus, who leads the way, though I stagger behind. I continue to believe, despite the inconsistency of my own heart, because Jesus walked the walk.

Finally, as a therapist, a pastor, and a professor, I've been privileged to lead a few others along the way. I've seen them find God in wilderness places despite excruciating pain, profound confusion, and moments of desperately wanting to return to Egypt. This book was written, in large part, on courage borrowed from these wilderness sojourners. Their names and identifying features have been changed to protect their privacy.

San Francisco
July 2011

Introduction

In the summer of 1997, I had the opportunity to study in Oxford, England. It was one of those magical summers, the kind you don't want to end. I traveled to historic sites around England. I studied with Dr. Crispin Fletcher-Louis, who I've since fallen out of touch with, but who gave me the gift of a scholarly spanking every now and then, followed by the sensitive care of one who sensed my anxiety. I ate and drank in the great pubs of the city, including the Eagle and Child, the now famous meeting place of the Inklings, an extraordinary group including C. S. Lewis, J. R. R. Tolkein, and Charles Williams. I visited The Kilns, C. S. Lewis's home while he resided in Oxford. Each day I researched in the basement of the Bodleian Library, which opened in 1620 and smells like it. But perhaps more personally significant than anything else, I took a class from Alister McGrath, who planted a seed that would blossom into this book.

Professor McGrath is well-known as one of the great living theologians today, but this great theologian, I found, is no stuffy British intellectual. He approaches the Bible with a kind of emotional and spiritual openness because it is the story out of which he is living his own life. He often talked about life as a journey, and how we are modern-day pilgrims navigating our own journeys, our own storylines.

While each person's story is unique, there's also a sense in which it's not. There are bigger stories, great metanarratives in which our stories find meaning and illumination. Over and over, McGrath would invite us to see our own journey as it is mirrored in the one great story of Scripture. He talked about how our lives today are re-narrated by the biblical story. While these ways of understanding the relationship of the great story of the Bible to the story of our individual lives has since become almost normative, these were heady new concepts for me.

Several years later, McGrath published a small book called *The Journey*. I liked it so much that I assigned it each year to my students in a seminary course called "Psychology in Relation to Theology"—and that is where I began to develop the idea of this book. McGrath writes,

> *The Exodus tells our story.* Each of us has a personal journey to make, from our own Egypt to our promised land. We have left something behind in order to make this journey. We have had to break free from our former lives in order to begin afresh. *We* were in Egypt. *We* were delivered from bondage. *We* are in the wilderness, on our way to the promised land. The story of the Exodus *involves* us—because it is *about* us. [1]

McGrath's little book is written from the perspective of a theologian, so it leans heavily on persons and experiences from church history. While I'm a theologian as well, my life's work has taken me in the direction of spiritual and practical theology. My academic work was in the area of psychology, and my work experience includes a fluid (sometimes jarring) blend of therapist, pastor, seminary professor, and writer. But perhaps the most influential part of the development of this book has been my students. Since 2003 at Reformed Theological Seminary in Orlando, I have taught a course that covers the contents of this book. Interacting with my students has been humbling, refining, challenging, and extremely invigorating. All the stories I've heard over the years in classrooms and therapy sessions make me a conduit for many different voices that speak in this book. Theologians and biblical scholars, psychologists and social workers, clinicians and pastors, stay-at-home moms and divorced dads, abuse victims and pornography addicts—these are the people whose stories interact with the biblical story that moves from Egypt to the promised land.

I have come to believe that the Exodus story deeply reflects all our stories, and it is my prayer that you will see how it reflects and illuminates your story as well. This book is an invitation to recognize that the Exodus is your story.

In Part 1—Egypt: Facing Our Fear, we'll explore the terrain of Egypt, seeing both its enslavement and its appeal. We'll explore how we long for very good things and how these things often enslave us. Often we reach for quick fixes, Band-Aids for deep wounds, only to be disappointed. God's remedy is a relational one. At its heart is the struggle to trust others, and, most important, to trust in God. Trust is the only way we can survive in the wilderness.

In Part 2—Sinai: Receiving Our New Identity, we'll explore the significance of Sinai. It's the first major stop in the wilderness, and it's both a signpost to a better life and a potential roadblock for those who aren't ready for the test. As travelers, we're tempted to pitch our tent at Sinai, unwilling to venture into the deeper, darker wilderness territory. Sinai represents our tendency to find both intellectual and moral certainty in our confusion. Growth requires us to travel on, to see Sinai as an invitation to pursue a life of shalom, of flourishing.

Part 3—Wilderness: Entering the Furnace of Transformation, is the core of the book. In the wilderness we're faced with our worst nightmares and our greatest possibilities. Though American culture holds out the hope of a quick fix, a microwavable spirituality, we'll see how God uses the wilderness to deepen us, to mature us, and to draw us into honest, authentic relationship with him as he continues to travel alongside us. We'll see that this is the journey Jesus took too.

Finally, we emerge from the wilderness. Part 4—Home: Experiencing New Identity and Mission, invites us to surrender through the image of open hands and to find rest in Jesus. Surrender leads us to life experienced in relationship with others, life manifested in happiness and virtue. We'll explore the Beatitudes as an announcement and invitation into the kingdom life of Jesus. But we'll also see that as quickly as we emerge, we find ourselves battling again with our memories of Egypt. This cyclical journey, this continuing battle, humbles us, leading us to increasing trust in the only successful Exodus journey ever taken—the wilderness journey of Jesus.

So jump in. Fasten your seatbelt. It's a wild ride, and not for the weak of heart. It would be convenient to avoid it, fight it, or resign to Egypt's snare. But it's well worth the ride. And in the end, we may say with the apostle Paul, "As for you, always be sober, endure suffering, do the work of an evangelist, carry out your ministry fully. As for me, I am already being poured out as a libation, and the time of my departure has come. I have fought the good fight, I have finished the race, I have kept the faith" (2 Timothy 4:5-7).

Part 1

*

Egypt:
Facing Our
Fear

Chapter 1

The Womb Becomes a Tomb

We have all read in scientific books, and indeed, in all romances, the story of the man who has forgotten his name. This man walks about the streets and can see and appreciate everything; only he cannot remember who he is. Well, every man is that man in the story. Every man has forgotten who he is.

—*G. K. Chesterton*

But now I realize that the real sin is to deny God's first love for me, to ignore my original goodness. Because without claiming that first love and that original goodness for myself, I lose touch with my true self and embark on a destructive search among the wrong people and in the wrong places for what can only be found in the house of my Father.

—*Henri Nouwen*

***

Are we not slaves?

All of us, to be sure, sometimes feel trapped in circumstances and situations that seem to exist beyond our control. But often we are also slaves to ourselves, trapped in patterns of thinking and feeling that stifle our freedom. Are we not all slaves?

The Exodus story would answer yes. We are all slaves. We're slaves to image and appearance, to substances and relationships, to compulsive behaviors and abusive systems. We're all ensnared by the Egypts in our lives and the pharaohs that demand our allegiance. As free as we might imagine ourselves, each of us continues to wrestle with the "old self" (Colossians 3:9), as the apostle called it, parts of us that have never left the slavery of Egypt for the flourishing we're made for.

Are we not slaves? This question may also have been difficult to answer for the Israelites living in Egypt those many years after the famine that brought them there in the first place. For years the Israelites found safety, security, and refuge in Egypt. Life in Egypt began with great hope and possibility. Many might have said, "We're not slaves at all! God has given us a good life here."

Such is the case with slavery. It's hard to leave Egypt. It was hard then. And it's hard now.

Parting Is Such Sweet Sorrow

Why is leaving Egypt so hard, after all? Why is liberation such a difficult journey?

The reality is that our enslavements are not all bad. There is a certain appeal even to our greatest vices. I once worked with a gambler who loved the adventure and risk. As much as he wanted to be free of his obsession, he felt a simultaneous passion for it. "I love gambling," he told me. "It wrecks everyone and everything around me, but in the moment there is no greater pleasure."

A friend of mine who is a financial analyst had a similar experience in her work habits. Though she's been called a workaholic by those who know her, and though she knows that her habits negatively impact her health and her relationships, she finds it hard to stop. "I cannot take a break. If I miss even the slightest change in the market, I lose my edge and my analysis is flawed."

What makes these enslavements of Egypt so powerful in our lives is that they connect to good desires built into us by the Creator, or else they would not be so enslaving. My client loved the adventure of gambling. Likewise, my friend loved the feeling of life on the edge. And I could understand both. We human beings were made for adventure and risk, in the image of our adventurous, risk-taking God. We were modeled for demanding, exacting, absorbing work in the image of our hard-working God.

Egypt was not always a place of slavery. Originally it was the place the Israelites were protected from famine and where they flourished. Our own Egypt experiences are the same. Good desires and longings somehow turn into enslavements. How does that happen?

In his penetrating essay "The Weight of Glory," C. S. Lewis helps us understand those good desires beneath our Egypt experiences. All his life he was enthralled and haunted by the memory of beauty and the search for it. It was the center of his life, his god. Beauty is, of course, a good thing, but he mistook beautiful things for beauty itself. Lewis writes,

> These things—the beauty, the memory of our own past—are good images of what we really desire; but if they are mistaken for the thing itself, they turn into dumb idols, breaking the hearts of their worshippers.

For they are not the thing itself; they are only the scent of a flower we have not found, the echo of a tune we have not heard, news from a country we have never yet visited.[1]

Good images of what we really desire. I like that. It rings true as I think about my own experiences. But it also rings true with the original story.

Desire beneath the Destruction

Lewis grasped the reality that good things in life often hold the paradoxical possibility of beauty and brokenness. So too Jewish mystical writers tend to grasp the dual role that Egypt plays in that central Jewish story, the Exodus. It's a space for growth and flourishing. But it can also be a trap if seen as the final destination. For the Israelites, it held the possibility of beauty and brokenness.

Interestingly, the metaphor that embraces this dual reality is that of a womb. The womb, of course, is a place for a baby to grow and be nurtured, a place of security and sustenance. But a womb is not a permanent home. At full term, the womb becomes a constrictive place where growth is no longer possible. So it was for the Israelites in Egypt. Estelle Frankel, a psychotherapist who works out of the Jewish mystical tradition, notes that the Hebrew word for Egypt, *Mitzrayim*, hints at a similar word in the Hebrew, *meitzarim*. What is fascinating is that this second word can be translated as "a narrow place," a space that is ultimately constricting. Just as the womb becomes an inhospitable place for a baby at full term to grow and thrive, so the once-fertile land of Egypt became an inhospitable place where the Israelites could no longer grow and prosper.[2] The womb became a tomb.

The experiences of most men and women I counsel resonate with this imagery. They wonder how the good things they've pursued in their lives have become traps, snares, obstacles to growth. To be sure, there is something soothing, comforting, even secure about Egypt's womb. I've watched women in abusive relationships as they have returned to an abuser over and over or found a relationship with another abusive man. These relationships are clearly destructive. But these women have another perspective. They have told me, time and again, that since abuse is what they know best, it is strangely familiar, even comforting. Returning to the abuser is like returning to the womb.

The inevitable question is what kind of good desire stands behind a horrible trap like abuse? Can it be that something good always hides behind some twisted form of slavery?

Women who have been abused will say that they long for security and find it in the perceived "strength" of the abusive man. Their good desire for love, for security, for comfort, for strength, or for intimacy becomes twisted and distorted. An abusive man is a womb that becomes a tomb.

This story of distorted, twisted goodness goes all the way back to the Garden of Eden, and it's been told countless times since, right up into your life and mine. You and I take good things and twist them. We ourselves become twisted in the process. It's a story of desire, good desire, but desire never completely satisfied. Gerald May writes,

There is a desire within each of us, in the deep center
of ourselves that we call our heart. We were born with
it, it is never completely satisfied, and it never dies.
We are often unaware of it, but it is always awake.[3]

It's this same desire that C. S. Lewis so often spoke about
as a longing that tugs at our hearts. What I hope to convey
to each person I work with is that their everyday struggles
with addiction, idolatry, or enslavement of any kind represent a kind of search for goodness, for life, for home. I hope
to awaken in them an insight into their original design, their
original goodness, which has now become so distorted. Only
then will they embrace their God-blessed, God-loved self, and
find the strength to leave Egypt, the womb that has become a
tomb. And that is the hardest battle of all.

Design Flaw

I recently read something appalling in a Christian publication.
A person claiming to have expertise in sexual addiction wrote
that sex addicts need to know that they are perverted human
beings whose black hearts desire only to destroy and mutilate
anything good in God's creation. Sickened, I could not help
but think of the many sex addicts I know—male and female.
If this person knew anything about sex addiction, I thought,
he'd know that this is exactly what each one of them thinks
about him- or herself. And it is the very thing that perpetuates
continued addiction!

A voice within each of us incessantly repeats this very lie.
It tells us that we're flawed at our core. It speaks of perversion, darkness, and irreparable sin. I'm convinced that this is

the voice of Satan ("the accuser" in Hebrew), a primordial liar who seeks to re-narrate the Christian story his own way. It's the voice that appears time and again in Scripture, whether in the Garden as a serpent or in the wilderness with Jesus as one who promises what he can't deliver. It's a voice that tells us that we're a design flaw in God's good creation.

I'm a Calvinist, and Calvinists famously believe that we're all a mess—it's called total depravity. But Calvinists also believe that God made the world—and us—good, in fact, *very* good (Genesis 1:31). We can only grasp the doctrine of original sin (that sin has infected everything and everyone) if we first grasp original goodness (that we were all created good and in God's image).

That's not to say that the deep sense of guilt that haunts our lives is unnecessary or wrong. Certainly much of what I see is bad guilt, sending the message "Nothing good can come from you" to our heart. But there is an important sense in which guilt can be a good thing. Guilt is our internal warning system that something in us that God made for good has veered off to the path to destruction.

Sin's real devastation, writes Henri Nouwen, is in its strange capacity to erase our memories, to cause us to forget our noble origins. "[T]he real sin is to deny God's first love for me, to ignore my original goodness. Because without claiming that first love and that original goodness for myself, I lose touch with my true self and embark on a destructive search among the wrong people and in the wrong places for what can only be found in the house of my Father."[4] And this is precisely what happened to the Israelites in Egypt. They were the descendants of Abraham, Isaac, and Jacob, people of the covenant. That was their true story. But slowly and steadily, over the span of four centuries, a different story began to form their identity: the Egyptian story, one that would plague them in their future journey.

Egypt is a place where we forget our noble roots as image-bearers created in goodness. We forget that we are born in and for love. That original destiny gets twisted into lesser loves and desire. Over the course of time, we develop a kind of spiritual amnesia. And at our lowest point, we ask, "Who am I?"

It's a recurring story among the people I work with:

* An addict is exposed after years of hiding and deceiving. His family is devastated. He says, "I don't know who I've become. This isn't me."

* A wealthy shopaholic is caught in the act of stealing, her only form of adventure in a predictable world. Still she asks, "Who am I?"

* An executive works fifteen hours a day. Barely awake, he says to me, "Chuck, I'm completely lost."

* A diabetic who can't stay away from sweets feels torn in his identity. "Part of me knows that I'm killing myself, but I don't care."

* A forty-something woman cannot stop going back for more plastic surgery. She tells me, "I'll keep working on me until I find the me I'm happy with."

* An accountant cannot stop doctoring the books at work, though at home and at church he's considered the good guy. "I don't know who I become when I'm doing that," he says.

Identity erodes as ordinary people literally lose themselves in their personal Egypts, forgetting who they are. As G. K. Chesterton says: "We have all read in scientific books, and indeed, in all romances, the story of the man who has forgotten his name. This man walks about the streets and can see and appreciate everything; only he cannot remember who he is. Well, every man is that man in the story. Every man has forgotten who he is."[5]

If you stick around Egypt, you lose your true story, and sooner or later, you'll come to believe that you are a design flaw.

On the Side of the Victim

Terrorism involves the use of brutal, random violence to bring people into a state of helplessness. There can also be a kind of terrorism of the soul. Pharaoh's agenda is clear. He wants to convince Israel that it is in their best interests to stay right where they are. He'll get that message across in whatever way he needs to.

Israel's love affair with Egypt began innocently, or so it seemed. Egypt was their brave protector in the midst of famine; one of their own, Joseph, presided over the whole business. But over time, a subtle change took place. Soon enough, Israel was hearing what all abusers tell their victims: Look at all I've done for you! You owe me!

And when psychological manipulation doesn't work, brutal force often does. In the days of Moses, Pharaoh was a paranoid abuser who stooped to genocide to protect his power. He stopped at nothing to keep the Israelites under his thumb.

I can imagine a conversation playing out with Moses that sounds a whole lot like the serpent playing his mind games with Adam and Eve, and with Jesus in the wilderness: "Moses, surely God hasn't promised you a land flowing with milk and honey? That's just like him—all talk and no action! Let me tell you where the action is. It's right here, working for me, enjoying the fruits of my empire. You've found happiness here, you and your people. Haven't my predecessors and I been good to you? Things can be good again if you just cooperate. Stick with what is certain. Don't believe those fairy tales of a better life!"

This is the psychological terrorism of Egypt. Slowly but surely we become numb to the true, the good, the beautiful. Eventually we forget that we were made for more.

In one of my favorite movies of all time, *The Shawshank Redemption*, a long-time prisoner named Red explains the psychology of prison to his friend Andy, who persistently dreams beyond the walls. "These walls are funny. First you hate 'em, then you get used to 'em. Enough time passes, you get so you depend on them. That's institutionalized. They send you here for life, and that's exactly what they take. The part that counts, anyway." Though Andy has been in prison for years, he has not forgotten life outside. He has not forgotten who he is. He says, "There's something inside . . . that they can't get to, that they can't touch. That's yours."[6]

Red is personally responsible for being in prison; his crimes left victims. But in another sense he is a victim. In this sense, it can be said that all of us are victims. We're victims of the deceit of Pharaoh. We're victims of the enslaving institutionalization that traps us in every form of Egypt we struggle

with. That's why Paul repeatedly calls us "slaves to sin" in
Romans 6.

Understanding this is especially important for Christians
who have been told, over and again, that sin is always our fault.
I don't want to minimize responsibility; the Exodus journey
compels us to deal with our hearts in deep ways. But the Exodus story also reminds us that there are powers outside of us
seeking our enslavement. While I'm suspicious of those who
find a demon under every bush to blame for a problem, I'm
equally suspicious of those who dismiss the ongoing and sin-
ister influence of that ancient serpent.

C. S. Lewis's *Screwtape Letters* is a series of fictional letters
written by a devil called Screwtape to his nephew, Worm-
wood. Screwtape is out to teach his young nephew how to
enslave his assigned human victim and snatch him away from
the Enemy (God). Here the ploy is pleasure:

> Never forget that when we are dealing with any
> pleasure in its healthy and normal and satisfying form,
> we are, in a sense, on the Enemy's ground. I know
> we have won many a soul through pleasure. All the
> same, it is His invention, not ours. He made all the
> pleasures: all our research so far has not enabled us
> to produce one. All we can do is to encourage the
> humans to take pleasures which our Enemy has pro-
> duced, at times, or in ways, or in degrees, which He
> has forbidden. Hence we always try to work away
> from the natural condition of any pleasure to that in
> which it is least natural, least redolent of its Maker,
> and least pleasurable.[7]

In every situation I see as a therapist and a pastor, I assume that Evil has set its target for destruction. What we call sin is something far more complex than we often think. When I see the businessman trapped in a pattern of stealing and deception, I'm not immediately interested in calling him to account by merely pointing to his sin. Sin is a far more complex reality. As Lewis reminds us, it's ultimately being separated from our Creator and losing our identity. It's not just about sins, but a sin-complex, at the heart of which lurks a monstrous deception.

At some level we're all victims. God doesn't start blaming the Israelites for getting themselves into the mess in Egypt. Instead, God rescues—without qualification, without interrogation. It's the pattern that emerges throughout the biblical story—the beautiful pattern of grace. He tells you and me that we're victims. We've been enslaved, so it's all right to cry out in frustration and pain. It's all right to feel lost and hopeless.

But it's also all right to hope. Moses is there to remind us that victims hope and pray and cry out. And God responds.

Out of Egypt

I feel trapped. That's one consistent message I hear from so many people. People feel trapped in jobs. They feel trapped in bad relationships. They feel trapped in family patterns. They feel trapped in a body they dislike. They feel trapped by their income, whether large or small. They feel trapped by having kids or by not having kids. They feel trapped in their singleness or in their bad marriages.

In a country that boasts the greatest freedom in the world, so many feel trapped, enslaved, stuck in a life that does not feel right. I'm not just talking about "those people"—the folks who need interventions and hospitalizations and jail time. I'm talking about you and me. I'm talking about businesspeople and stay-at-home moms and pastors and plumbers.

Are you ready to take this spiritual geography seriously? Are you ready to see that this story is about *you*? I'm pretty sure people who are in abusive relationships will resonate with the basic message of this book. I'm pretty sure people who are addicted to porn, or eating, or cutting will see it too. But I'm also interested in the person who has it all, but secretly fears that it's all not enough.

The Exodus journey is for each and every person; we all need a liberator, a Savior.

In fact, Jesus himself took the journey. Many years after the Exodus, a young boy was born in Bethlehem. An evil and paranoid tyrant called Herod decided to go on a child-hunt of his own, much as Egypt's Pharaoh had many years earlier.

> Now after they had left, an angel of the Lord appeared to Joseph in a dream and said, "Get up, take the child and his mother, and flee to Egypt, and remain there until I tell you; for Herod is about to search for the child, to destroy him." Then Joseph got up, took the child and his mother by night, and went to Egypt, and remained there until the death of Herod. This was to fulfill what had been spoken by the Lord through the prophet, "Out of Egypt I have called my son."
>
> —Matthew 2:13-15

Out of Egypt. Every original Jewish reader seeing this in Matthew's gospel would have known exactly what this meant. They'd understand that Jesus was pioneering the long-awaited new Exodus that would lead an exiled and enslaved people into the long-awaited promised land. Everyone who had experienced the hardship of slavery would find hope.

This is your story and this is my story. Our Exodus road has been paved by Jesus himself. Are you ready to leave Egypt?

Discussion

1. Read Exodus 1. Notice the shift from Israel growing and thriving to Pharaoh's persecution. What do you suppose provoked Pharaoh's wrath?

2. How is your story mirrored in Exodus 1? How does this chapter speak to your journey?

3. Think of some good thing that has become misdirected in your life. Perhaps it's a good desire for influence that has turned into workaholism, or a love for good food that has turned into overeating. What good thing behind these things might you be longing for?

4. How do you relate to the excerpt from *The Shawshank Redemption*? How have you become "institutionalized"?

5. How does it make you feel to know that Jesus has also taken the Exodus journey?

Chapter 2

Band-Aids in Prison

*P*rophets and priests and everyone in between twist words
  and doctor truth. My people are broken—shattered!—and
they put on Band-Aids, saying, "It's not so bad. You'll be just
fine." But things are not "just fine"!

—Jeremiah 6:13, The Message

*To allow oneself to be carried away by a multitude of con-
flicting concerns, to surrender to too many demands, to
commit oneself to too many projects, to want to help
everyone in everything, is to succumb to violence.*

—*Thomas Merton*

***

I remember meeting briefly with Beth one December after she
nearly melted down in a rehearsal for the church Christmas
program. A few of her friends had warned me that she was
on the brink again. We had seen this cycle before. She'd ramp
up for the holidays, frantically tackling the Christmas program, the children's Lessons and Carols, and the Angel Tree.
Beth was an extraordinary servant producing an extraordinary

program. We all loved her. But like clockwork, somewhere in those pressure-packed days, she would crash.

I knew Beth's patterns well enough to suspect that she was not only running hard, but also running away from something. I wasn't sure what. I suspect she knew that something was up when I asked her to stop by my office one afternoon. After a bit of small talk about her kids and holiday plans, I told her that I had something important to ask her.

She sat up straight, as if waiting for a blow.

"Besides all of your ministries taking a big hit from the loss of your leadership, what would happen if you simply stopped, passed the work to someone else, and rested?" I said.

She knew exactly what I was getting at.

"Really, Chuck? Stop? If I stopped, I'd have to *feel*."

Stockholm Syndrome of the Soul

As I write this, Elizabeth Smart's abductor is on trial in Utah. Her tragic story became national news. Abducted at the age of fourteen, she was kidnapped from her home and held for almost a year by Brian David Mitchell and his wife, Wanda Barzee. What puzzled some was that Smart seemed to have opportunities to escape, or at least to alert others about her captivity. Yet she didn't. Why?

Since the infamous 1974 abduction of Patty Hearst, psychologists have made a compelling case for a condition called "Stockholm syndrome." While it might seem that survival instinct would cause a person to fight back, some who are abducted react in just the opposite way. They appease their captors, even ingratiate themselves to them, for the sake of survival. Makes sense, right?

Many don't think so. I remember watching a popular cable news channel one night when a group of so-called experts discussed the legitimacy of Stockholm syndrome. One of them completely dismissed Smart's experience. Though I don't remember his exact words, he said something like this: "Smart is a liar! She wanted to be abducted, she wanted sex, and she certainly never wanted to return home."

This "expert" must not have read the Exodus story.

Let's be honest. There was a whole lot about Egypt to like. After all, the Israelites had settled there for hundreds of years. They'd built houses and become accustomed to the highways and back roads of Egypt. Egypt had become home.

And yet we wince with disbelief each time we see the Israelites rebel against Moses, threatening to return to the place of their captivity. With our thousands of years of hindsight, we assume we'd make the better choice. But would we?

Stockholm syndrome is all about coping, and coping is what we do to get through life's rough places. Faced with the familiar places of Egypt in our own lives, we choose to stay and survive. We find ways to make slavery more palatable.

I was talking to a friend the other day about her work environment. About a year ago she'd told me that it had become tough to endure the "locker room" atmosphere. Surrounded by a throng of male coworkers, she received every sexually explicit email, overheard conversations about the previous evening's sexual exploits, and even found herself a victim of their racy comments. She often felt embarrassed and self-conscious. This time she described her situation differently. "It's like white noise, Chuck," she told me. "I hardly hear it." But when I asked a few more questions, I discovered that the atmosphere was even worse; the comments directed toward her were more frequent and direct. All it took was a little empathy from me for her to begin to cry. It was clear to me that it was definitely not white noise.

For my friend, slavery had become normal. Or so she thought. In reality, she'd been daily bandaging some significant soul wounds. But her survival strategy was taking a toll. She suspected that she was becoming more depressed and told me that her roommates commented that she was always on edge. My friend was experiencing the slow constriction of slavery. Together we decided that mere survival was no longer an option.

I suspect that each of us can relate to her story in some way. Why do we succumb to this soul-sucking form of Stockholm syndrome? Why is it so difficult at times to take our slavery seriously?

Band-Aid Theology

The prophet Jeremiah indicted the leaders of his day as Band-Aid theologians who minimized the reality of their slavery. They had abandoned the "ancient paths" (Jeremiah 6:16) for the quick fixes and ephemeral therapies of the day. Even the most respected among them—the pastors—had bought into a theology of pain minimization and management. Eugene Peterson's paraphrase is priceless: "Prophets and priests and everyone in between twist words and doctor truth. My people are broken—shattered!— and they put on Band-Aids, saying, 'It's not so bad. You'll be just fine.' But things are not 'just fine'!" (Jeremiah 6:13, *The Message*).

I'll often tell my students that much of what we call "therapy" these days amounts to a kind of Band-Aid theology. We'll look at the major orientations—cognitive-behavioral, rational-emotive, gestalt, psychodynamic, family systems—only to discover that the way each one conceives of the problem and articulates a response is too narrow, too simplistic. One student saw a Christian cognitive-behavioral therapist who addressed her struggles with self-image and food as a self-talk issue. "We need to change the way you talk to yourself," she told her. "Therapy is about reprogramming your negative thoughts with positive thoughts." There was no exploration of my student's story, no interest in seeing the issues in the larger context of a whole life. My student said, "I felt like a computer being reprogrammed." That is not to say that these forms of therapy are not at all helpful. As a therapist, I'm influenced by each one. But too much of it is Band-Aids on gaping wounds.

Then, in my class, we switch to looking at how pastors and churches respond to pain. Again, most of what I hear is that churches are much too hesitant in acknowledging the depth of pain and struggle in people's lives. One student recalled how her church dealt with the suicide of a popular teen in the youth group. Her pastor acknowledged people's sadness, but then immediately encouraged them to see God's purposes in this death, and to rejoice that this young man was with Jesus. So this student (and many others in the church) tucked away their pain.

For the most part, North American Christianity lacks a theology of suffering. We major in praise songs and minor in lament. When is the last time your church engaged in a corporate act of grieving? Instead, a kind of haloed optimism dominates, and many churches seem to grow because of their capacity to help people feel better about themselves. Yet Scripture unapologetically embraces the full range of human emotional experience. As Old Testament scholar Walter Brueggemann writes, Israel, at her best, knew how to trust God in the midst of deep pain.

> Israel unflinchingly saw and affirmed that life as it comes, along with its joys, is beset by hurt, betrayal, loneliness, disease, threat, anxiety, bewilderment, anger, hatred, and anguish. The study of lament may suggest a corrective to the euphoric, celebrative notions of faith that romantically pretend that life is sweetness and joy, even delight. It may be suggested that the one-sided . . . renewal of today has, in effect, driven the hurtful side of experience into obscure corners of faith practice or completely out of Christian worship.[1]

Band-Aid theology requires that you and I stuff our pain into internal compartments—just outside of our emotional awareness but still able to deeply impact us. Like the Israelites in Egypt, we live with a functional denial of our present reality. For Israel that reality was forced labor, genocide, and slavery. For us, in our technologically driven, 24/7 culture, it is a thousand different things. Band-Aids come in all shapes and sizes.

Or, we might compartmentalize our capacity for dealing with hurt. My wife, Sara, tells me that while I'm dedicated to being present and emotionally available to my clients, I'm often oblivious to my family's needs. Ripping off emotional Band-Aids from my clients, I'm busy applying them to the struggles of my own family.

Many times I've responded to a real struggle Sara is having with, "You're making too big a deal out of this." I'll dismiss it without a bit of curiosity. Frankly, sometimes it just feels easier. A person who attended a marriage conference I led said just this. He told me, "Chuck, I don't have the energy to do what you are suggesting. I'm barely able to keep twenty employees happy and productive."

I get it. I avoid, dismiss, minimize, deny, and bandage up better than most. I used to be a lot harder on others and myself for this. But I find that I'm on a trajectory of being a life-long Band-Aid theologian myself. This Exodus invitation, however, is not about journeying perfectly, as we'll see. It's about journeying honestly. An honest look at ourselves reveals that our hearts are addicted to managing our pain and sin rather than really acknowledging and embracing them. We cope rather than surrender. It takes the dark valleys of the wilderness to fully learn to live with spiritual courage and authenticity. But for now it's important to simply pay attention to your very own Egypt and how it operates in your life.

Cope

The people in a small group I led decided to pay closer attention to our coping mechanisms. It began as a very simple exercise. I didn't want to leave people with the impression that Egypt is only about major addictions or traumas, though that can certainly be the case. So I invited everyone to begin paying attention to the simple ways of coping and bandaging that happen day to day.

One person came back with a fairly simple observation. She copes with the turmoil of her home by being relentlessly helpful. She makes sure everyone and everything is taken care of. If she makes the lunches and cleans the rooms and stocks the refrigerator and irons the clothes, she reasons, then she'll not have to deal with the frustration of her demanding husband or the whining of her needy kids. "I cope by helping," she said.

Her insight sparked a recollection of a quote from Thomas Merton: "To allow oneself to be carried away by a multitude of conflicting concerns, to surrender to too many demands, to commit oneself to too many projects, to want to help everyone in everything is to succumb to violence."[2] As I read the woman began to tear up. When I asked what she was feeling, she said, "That describes me to a tee. But what is most disturbing was the last part about succumbing to violence. What am I doing to myself?"

This simple exercise opened up an opportunity for deeper reflection. That night our desire was not to fix or analyze our friend. We just listened. And so did her husband. Understanding his own complicity, he said, "Honey, I don't want you to continue to hurt yourself like this. I'm responsible, in large part, for creating this tension at home. I cope with a chaotic and busy life by expecting that you and everyone else will make sure I thrive. I'm sorry for doing this to you." They embraced in tears, and it became a moment of healing for a marriage that up to that point had been lifeless.

Another group member, a successful lawyer in his forties, felt exposed when this man spoke honestly about a busy and chaotic life. The following week he said, "What you don't know about me is that I am desperately afraid of failing. I'm determined to be seen as a success. But I'm really, really tired." Once again, the group rallied around the honesty, urging him to continue to uncover the wound beneath the Band-Aid.

I'm convinced that the enslaving Evil One hates moments like these. But this kind of relationship-building, life-giving honesty has the capacity to break through our coping and set us on the path to freedom.

Corporate sage and poet David Whyte speaks to his own tendency to use work and busyness as a coping mechanism. He writes:

> My work had become important to me in a subtly corrupting way. I ran the educational program in an organization dedicated to environmental teaching, and my scheduled busyness was a wonderful measure of my self-importance. I felt as if I was affecting hundreds of people directly and thousands of people indirectly. I therefore felt it was worth killing myself a little for it.[3]

A similar theme emerges in both Merton's and Whyte's analysis. Merton calls it "succumbing to violence." Whyte sees it as killing himself a little. Both are gruesome metaphors. We cannot merely point to the addict or the abused and say, "They're screwed up and their behavior will eventually kill them." If Merton and Whyte are right, we're doing the same thing in our everyday choices to be chronically helpfully or pathologically busy.

In our small group something began to change. By speaking to the reality of our ordinary ways of coping with enslavements, we began to see Egypt for what it really is—a prison, a tomb, a death chamber. We didn't change overnight or become instant spiritual giants. In fact, we continued to struggle and battle. But we did it more honestly—and we did it together, which was, perhaps, the most important part.

Whether we're struggling with garden-variety compulsions such as helping or workaholism or are neck-deep in self-destructive behavior, we all need an honest moment of self-realization. William Cope Moyers, the son of political commentator and television host Bill Moyers, documented his story of addiction and recovery in his autobiography *Broken*. It's both a tragic and ironically fascinating story of a man who chose to live through his middle name instead of his given first name. It's a story of man who refused to take seriously how radically trapped, addicted, and enslaved he was, a man who applied Band-Aids to deep soul wounds.

After "hitting bottom" time after time, he finally woke up. And as many addicts do, he asked himself questions about why he'd refused to take his addiction seriously before then. Facing reality squarely for the first time, he wonders what would have happened had he "willingly accepted [his] new identity as William the alcoholic and crack cocaine addict, finally shedding the illusion that I could 'cope' with life?"[4]

Ordinary Addicts

If we're ready to face the way that Egypt has enslaved us, then perhaps we're ready to take another step and recognize that we are addicts too. Perhaps not in the clinical sense, but in the sense that we tend to cope with life in ways that bring some level of violence and death to us. Gerald May, one of the greatest experts on addiction, writes

> I am not being flippant when I say that all of us suffer from addiction. Nor am I reducing the meaning of addiction. I mean in all truth that the psychological, neurological, and spiritual dynamics of full-fledged addiction are actively at work within every human being. The same processes that are responsible for addiction to alcohol and narcotics are also responsible for addiction to ideas, work, relationships, power, moods, fantasies, and an endless variety of other things. We are all addicts in every sense of the word. Moreover, our addictions are our own worst enemies. They enslave us with chains that are of our own making and yet that, paradoxically, are virtually beyond our control. Addiction also makes idolaters of us all, because it forces us to worship these objects of attachment, thereby preventing us from truly, freely loving God and one another.[5]

Most of us are probably more comfortable with the language of idolatry that May uses rather than the language of addiction. We talk about the idols of money or power or sex fairly comfortably. But taking this to the level of addiction requires us to see the full effects of Egypt in our lives. It challenges us to see the full impact of our Band-Aid solutions.

Let's take a simple example. In 2010, Facebook surpassed Google for the most web activity. Many of us are now keeping track of old friends, high-school classmates, former girlfriends and boyfriends, and second or third cousins through the social network. Just the other day a coworker mentioned that he and his wife spend huge amounts of time on Facebook. In the evenings they often check in on Facebook, chatting with old friends, uploading new pictures and updates from their lives, and enjoying some of the fun new features it offers.

One evening, they returned home to find that their Internet connection had died. They quickly searched for other networks to no avail. "I could feel my heart beginning to race a bit," my friend said. His wife began doing the dishes. She was silent, clearly irritated. And then it dawned on my friend. "We're addicts!" he said. "Look at us. We're anxious, angry, irritated, trying to find something to fill the void." He got it. My friend saw that ordinary things can do the same things psychologically and physiologically, on a smaller level, as severe addictions.

Gerald May continues, "Psychologically, addiction uses up desire. It is like a psychic malignancy sucking our life energy into specific obsessions and compulsions, leaving less and less energy available for other people and other pursuits."6 This is exactly what was happening to my friends. Lost in the world of Facebook, their energy was sucked into their addiction, leaving less for their relationship. They were coexisting in front of their laptops while sitting on the couch next to one another, hardly engaging with each other.

I can name at least a dozen of these ordinary addictions in my own life. All I need to do is begin to think about what impacts me when I lose it or miss it. My iPhone may top the list. Having "lost" it in the couch several times, the level of panic that invades my body is disturbing. Then there is Saturday and Sunday football, particularly when I miss my favorite games. Health is another. I become edgy and uneasy when my ability to be productive is taken away. Coffee is an obvious one. If I miss my first cup, my brain tells me my day will be awful. Even taking a shower is up there. I just cannot operate without one. It's why I despise camping.

You may be thinking I've gone over the edge here, finding addictions everywhere. But follow the trajectory of these simple daily attachments and you'll find a need for security, for safety, for intimacy, for connection, for regularity, for productivity. Go a bit deeper and you'll find that each of these things can even replace God, providing for my needs without consideration of my deep and desperate neediness as a human being. Each can be a way of coping, a reality-denying form of self-preservation that robs me of grace.

I'm certainly not saying that coffee, technology, health, and family are bad. I'm convinced, though, that we fail to take seriously how spiritually, psychologically, emotionally, and physiologically dependent we are on all kinds of ordinary things. When we're unaware of the impact of these kinds of ordinary attachments in our lives, we might miss the truth of our own enslavements. All together, these things can contribute to that psychological reality of "institutionalization" that Red ruminated on in *The Shawshank Redemption*.

As we'll see in the next chapter, this is why God gave Israel Moses. We all need a Moses—someone who's willing to wake us up to the larger invitation God offers of life, freedom, beauty, love, desire, and goodness.

Beth, my collapsing Christmas dynamo, wasn't happy when she left my office that day. Working for the church gave her some sense of joy, but what became apparent was that it also gave her relief from a more profound pain that seemed to subside when she was busily serving others. She knew that stepping away from leadership meant that she would have to feel, and that these feelings would not be pleasant. Serving the church, in fact, was Beth's addiction, her soul's strategy for survival. It mitigated the awful sense of guilt she carried for years.

Beth entered therapy that January. In March she came back to my office for a visit. "Thanks for telling me to quit, Chuck," she said. I was surprised. She explained that service to the church was the only way her family managed to stay together when she was young. Her father was an elder. Her mother led the choir. Everyone served—in large part because life at home was hell. Her parents' marriage had been arranged without their consent by two very influential Southern families, and they had always resented it. Instead of honestly facing their hurt, they determined to make things work. Their outlet became the church, and their kids became products of a dysfunctional system of avoiding pain by serving others.

Beth visited her mother and father shortly after that for an honest conversation about her past. Though it was difficult, her mother and father understood, at least in part. Beth wasn't sure whether it came from their uncanny ability to do the right "Christian" thing, but both asked for forgiveness. Beth left, feeling released from a prison of forty years.

"No more Band-Aids, Chuck," she said.

When Beth emerged once again as a leader in the church, it was clear that she was free from the shackles of Egypt.

Discussion

1. What does Egypt signify? What does Egypt signify in your own story?

2. Can you relate to the metaphor of Stockholm syndrome? In what ways has it played out in the lives of people you know? In your own life?

3. What Band-Aids in your life allow you to cope? Can you identify with any of the "ordinary addictions" in this chapter?

4. What would "leaving Egypt" mean for you? You may not have a full answer yet, but begin thinking of which Egypts in your life might be tougher to leave, and which ones might be easier.

Chapter 3

A Moses for Our Journey

For they are a rebellious people,
faithless children,
children who will not hear
the instruction of the LORD;
who say to the seers, "Do not see";
and to the prophets, "Do not prophesy to us what is right;
speak to us smooth things,
prophesy illusions,
leave the way, turn aside from the path,
let us hear no more about the Holy One of Israel."
—Isaiah 30:9-11

It is a wonderful thing for a person to talk to those who speak
about this interior castle, to draw near not only to those seen
to be in these rooms where he is but to those known to have
entered the ones closer to the center . . . and he can converse so
much with them that they will bring him to where they are.[1]
—Teresa of Avila

✳✳✳

I was in a restaurant with some friends a few years back. It
was apparent very soon after we were seated that our service
would be brutal. As we sat down, one couple immediately

rose from their seats. I made eye contact with the woman as she grumbled under her breath, tossing two bucks on the table for a half glass of iced tea. A guy at the table behind us tapped my friend's shoulder and said, "Good luck getting anything to eat today. One waitress . . . and I think she's the cook too."

Looking distraught, the waitress returned with four salads and was greeted by applause from the booth beside ours. "Can I get a refill?" someone shouted from the other side of the restaurant. With a big sigh, she stepped to our booth, and, taking her pad from her apron, said, "I'm sorry guys. What can I get you to drink?"

We waited fifteen minutes for two Diet Cokes, a raspberry iced tea, and a water.

Very quickly I realized that we were forming a new bond over our difficult experience. Two of my buddies had also joined the chorus of praise and lament. "Hooray!" we'd shout if we saw her coming even remotely close to our table with food. "Aawww . . ." we'd cry, as she'd head instead for another customer. We all joined in—except for my friend Jamie.

"You see that manager over there?" he said. We hadn't noticed, having lost ourselves in the collective pity-party. A guy in a suit was leaning against the bar, looking up at a television tuned in to ESPN. "He hasn't moved in a half-hour."

Jamie is one of those guys who spots injustice like a mother hears her child cry in the night, a guy whose seriousness about injustice immediately retunes your own conscience. Suddenly we saw what Jamie saw—a waitress who was about to lose it in a sea of grumpy customers with no thought of anything but their appetite.

Then Jamie called her name.

"Rachael!" She was clearly surprised. She'd been referred to as "Ma'am," "You," "Miss," "Sweetie," "Stranger," and probably other unmentionables in the past hour, but not by her name. Not with dignity.

"I'm sorry . . ." she exclaimed, clearly waiting for another verbal lashing. But Jamie interrupted. "Rachael, it looks like you are having a tough day. Is that your boss?" he said, pointing toward the bar.

"Yes . . . and I completely understand that you want to talk to him. I'll get him right away."

"No, wait a moment, Rachael," Jamie said as she attempted to call to her manager. She returned dutifully. "Don't be sorry, Rachael. I'm sorry. I'm sorry he hasn't done a thing to help you. I'm sorry you've had to put up with all of us today. I just wanted you to know that."

Rachael took a deep breath in and then released it, losing a hundred pounds of emotional weight in the exhale. "Thank you," she said, walking away like a pardoned prisoner.

Drawn Out

The epic story of Moses has surprising relevance for those of us navigating our own journeys out of Egypt.

Pharaoh, it seems, was not at all interested in seeing the Israelites continue to flourish and multiply in the Genesis tradition as they were doing in Egypt (Exodus 1:12). So he published an edict: All newborn Israelite boys were to be thrown into the Nile (1:22). But Moses had a very crafty mother. She made sure he ended up in the Nile—with luxury accommodations.

Perhaps you know the rest of the story. Moses was launched into the Nile in a papyrus basket and rescued by Pharaoh's daughter, who was determined to raise this little "orphan" in the secure confines of the palace. Ironically, his care would be entrusted to his very own mother. His name—meaning "drawn out"—suggests his own story of being drawn out of the dangerous waters, but it also foreshadows the story of many, many others who would traverse unscathed through the Red Sea and be released into freedom. Moses would become the man God chose to invite an embattled, enslaved, and oppressed people into new life, to draw them out of darkness into light.

Moses and my friend Jamie have a lot in common. I see three main ways in which Moses and Jamie inspire us today, both in the kinds of mentors and counselors we seek in our lives and the kinds of mentors and counselors we seek to become to others. Both hated injustice and exposed it for what it was. Both saw dignity where others saw an opportunity for mockery. Finally, both had a vision for others that would inspire a new way of living and acting.

Exposing Injustice

What inspired me about Jamie's actions, in large part, is what he saw taking place behind the scenes. It takes vision to see what many of us either don't see or choose not to see. Let's face it, exposing injustice is inconvenient. It's messy. And often it's thankless.

The ten plagues were an extraordinary object lesson for Pharaoh and the Egyptians. It was as if God were saying through Moses, "Look at the extraordinary destruction of everything I have created good that comes when you abuse and oppress." Commentators have suggested that these were ten lessons in *un*creation. Through Moses God would show in ten vivid real-life illustrations what creation reversal looks like. All present would bear witness to God's hard-hitting lessons on the ramifications of injustice and oppression.

If you're like me, you might find this strategy a bit uncomfortable. I like the idea of God creating, restoring, redeeming, and blessing. The thought of a creation-reversing God scares me. But what may be scarier is a God who is oblivious to injustice. But that simply is not the God of the Exodus. This God sees injustice. This God acts on behalf of the oppressed. And when God is going after injustice, it's not wise to stand in the way.

Combating injustice may be as basic as Jamie's intervention into Rachael's situation. It did not come with a high cost. At other times, speaking to injustice can come at great personal cost. We see this in the lives of martyrs like Dietrich Bonhoeffer and Martin Luther King, Jr. But quite often, ordinary people take huge risks out of the public eye. I have some friends who work every day for victims of sexual assault and violence, for young girls caught in sex trafficking, for the homeless, and among prison inmates. Most of them make far less money for the emotionally demanding work they do than others with the same education and resume. Yet something compels them to return to those often thankless struggles day after day.

Engaging in this Moses-like work doesn't require a major career change, though. Sometimes, it merely requires an honest conversation over coffee. In my church, we train lay counselors to meet with people who might not want or need to speak with a trained therapist. One lay counselor told me recently, "My job is often to tell people, 'You don't need to live like this anymore.'" It's the courage to speak to the reality of Egypt in a person's life that makes the difference.

Proclaiming Dignity

Both Moses and Jamie recognized dignity when others saw depravity.

Jamie saw what the rest of us didn't or didn't choose to see at the restaurant. He saw a woman, not just a waitress. He used her name instead of calling her one. Jamie, I suspect, saw a woman with a story, while the rest of us couldn't see past her enslavement for that hour.

In *The Shawshank Redemption*, Andy Dufresne is a Moses figure who refuses to ignore injustice. After the fatal beating of a prisoner by a tyrant guard, Andy is seen eating with a few fellow prisoners who are talking about the murder. Andy asks a simple question: "What was his name?" The question evokes rage from another prisoner, who fires back, saying, "It doesn't . . . matter what his name was. He's dead."[2] By insisting on a name, Andy is laying claim to what little dignity may be available in an institution that seems to crush it.

Exodus tells the story of a God who sees his people mired in a death spiral of injustice and enslavement and rescues them, restoring them to dignity. The Exodus story is retold by Ezekiel in a way that casts Israel in the part of a naked and defenseless baby rescued, revived, and destined to become a queen. God's dignity project is in full color and on full display here:

As for your birth, on the day you were born y
cord was not cut, nor were you washed wi
to cleanse you, nor rubbed with salt, nor wra
cloths. No eye pitied you, to do any of these thi ͺͺ ɪ0r
you out of compassion for you; but you were thrown
out in the open field, for you were abhorred on the day
you were born. I passed by you, and saw you flailing
about in your blood. As you lay in your blood, I said
to you, "Live! and grow up like a plant of the field."
You grew up and became tall and arrived at full wom-
anhood; your breasts were formed, and your hair had
grown; yet you were naked and bare. I passed by you
again and looked on you; you were at the age for love. I
spread the edge of my cloak over you, and covered your
nakedness: I pledged myself to you and entered into a
covenant with you, says the Lord GOD, and you became
mine. Then I bathed you with water and washed off the
blood from you, and anointed you with oil. I clothed
you with embroidered cloth and with sandals of fine
leather; I bound you in fine linen and covered you with
rich fabric. I adorned you with ornaments: I put brace-
lets on your arms, a chain on your neck, a ring on your
nose, earrings in your ears, and a beautiful crown upon
your head. You were adorned with gold and silver,
while your clothing was of fine linen, rich fabric, and
embroidered cloth. You had choice flour and honey
and oil for food. You grew exceedingly beautiful, fit
to be a queen. Your fame spread among the nations on
account of your beauty, for it was perfect because of

my splendor that I had bestowed on you, says the Lord God (Ezekiel 16:4-14).

This is precisely how the Exodus story unfolds. In the Israelites, God does not see slaves. God sees a people he loves and with whom he has a covenant relationship. In other words, God sees deeply—beneath the pain, beneath the years of hardened slave labor, beneath the broken traditions. God sees Israel as his covenant children, once lost and now found. God sends Moses to call her by her name, Israel, reminding her that her identity is not as a slave but as God's own (Exodus 6:7). Israel is God's daughter, she is God's bride.

Some friends of ours adopted a little girl from Ethiopia a few years back. This little girl's journey began with abandonment and was marked by trauma. After months of painful bureaucratic legwork and medical complications, the adoption was finally completed. Arriving back home with their child, my friends wore the pain of all they had gone through. The roller-coaster adoption process with every imaginable complication had left them emotionally, spiritually, and physically exhausted. Yet the moment they introduced their child, a new name seemed to speak dignity into the exhausting, traumatic story. "I'd like to introduce you to Salem," my friend Josh said. *Salem.* Shalom. Peace.

In her memoir *Stumbling toward Faith*, Renee Altson tells a gruesome story some publishers were afraid to print for fear that it might not be believed. Raped by her own father as he recited the Lord's Prayer over her and abused by many others along the way, this extraordinary woman relentlessly committed herself to the painful process of healing needed to love her husband and child, and to love herself. At one point, talking to her therapist, she discovered that she could no longer live with her birth name. She asked for a new name and trusted that he might bless her with one. After some time, he came back with Renee. Reborn.

Both Salem and Renee experienced a Moses in their lives. Each was blessed with a new name and new dignity. Leaving Egypt involves leaving our old identities, rooted in the narrative of an abusive and destructive power. But we need help along the way. We need a Moses, a Jamie—someone to help us discover a new name, to help us form a new identity as free children of God. When someone enters into our brokenness with us, we begin to consider the awesome possibility that a promised land awaits.

Vision

Long ago, God told Moses to cast this vision for the Israelites:

> Say therefore to the Israelites, "I am the LORD, and I will free you from the burdens of the Egyptians and deliver you from slavery to them. I will redeem you with an outstretched arm and with mighty acts of judgment. I will take you as my people, and I will be your God. You shall know that I am the LORD your God, who has freed you from the burdens of the Egyptians. I will bring you into the land that I swore to give to Abraham, Isaac, and Jacob; I will give it to you for a possession. I am the LORD." Moses told this to the Israelites; but they would not listen to Moses,

because of their broken spirit and their cruel slavery (Exodus 6:6-9).

Here is a relentlessly committed God empowering Moses to cast a vision for hope, long-term hope, which would take them from the terror of slavery to the bliss of a land flowing with milk and honey. It's an extraordinary vision, a picture of a future beyond the present pain.

Let's face it, our hearts are moved when we're challenged to hope beyond our present struggles. Whether you incline to the left or to the right politically, you're almost certain to identify your favorite political leaders as those who saw beyond present struggles into a more optimistic future. Abraham Lincoln could see a world beyond slavery. Teddy Roosevelt could imagine a canal that would revolutionize trade, travel, and security. Ronald Reagan could envision a world lifted out from under the oppressive weight of communism. Barack Obama could sloganize "Hope" as a way out of political deadlock. We are moved by those who see a future we cannot see.

Moses saw a future that was unimaginable to the enslaved Israelite. The text tells us that the Israelites resisted Moses because of their "broken spirit" and their "cruel slavery." They'd been abused so long, institutionalized by their slavery so fully, that they had lost their capacity for a vision of hope.

At some point the pain is so intense, the indignity so deep, that our hearts simply give out and we give up—a state of resignation that leads us to shut our ears to whatever Moses, Jamie, or anyone else might tell us. Sometimes we are just too broken to hear and believe.

And yet God is relentless in casting a vision of hope for the Israelites. We are called to the same vision of relentless hopefulness in the lives of others.

In the six years I spent counseling Nell, she'd often ask, "Will I ever get beyond my fear of being betrayed again?" Like Renee, Nell had been sexually abused. At twenty-eight, she feared that she was too broken to ever marry, let alone date someone. "I can't imagine allowing a man to touch me in any way, ever," she'd say. I didn't want to convey the naïve optimism we so often see in churches today: "Don't worry, with God, anything is possible!" But I did want to cast a vision. So often I'd simply say, "I'm pretty convinced we'll both be crying and laughing on your wedding day . . . and you'd better ask me to perform the wedding!"

Hope is more than saying, "It will all be OK." As we'll see, suffering and struggle is very much a part of the journey toward freedom. But a hopeful vision dares to defy the voices of despair. In speaking of my client's wedding day, I was making no promise. Nor was I offering a clear, effortless path to victory. I was simply speaking to the ironic, surprising, and often unexpected grace of a God who sees a future beyond our painful present.

God's vision for Israel was a vision of dignity and of flourishing, fully aware of the reality of her long years of suffering. It was neither narrow nor naïve. In reality, I don't know what will happen in my clients' lives or even my own from one day to the next. We live in an uncertain world, and I've seen progress turn to despair time and again. But what we can be certain of is that God not only desires but is committed to bring about our flourishing. Though we do not make naïve promises, we can be bold in our embrace of God's present and future vision of a "land flowing with milk and honey" where Salem, Renee, Nell, and the rest of us will enjoy God's shalom.

I did perform Nell's wedding. And we did cry and laugh. Nell's marriage has been difficult at times. We expected as much. But she has grown more and more in her ability to see beyond her present pain and into a future of dignity and flourishing. She is living proof of the power of a hopeful vision.

Becoming a Moses

We all need a Moses for the journey. We need a Moses because we cannot do it alone. Life in Egypt breeds loneliness, fear, and isolation. But having a Moses in our life enables us to face our enslavements and casts a vision of hope.

A mentor named Roger played the role of Moses during several critical years of my life. Roger sat with me almost every week for three years with a kind of curiosity and compassion that I had never experienced before. He seemed to delight in my mundane stories. He remembered key names from my past. He anticipated how I'd react to different situations because he knew me so well. I don't think I've ever been known like that by anyone other than my wife. He was an extraordinary gift.

Over time, I no longer needed regular time with Roger. Very slowly God was calling and equipping me to become a Roger to others. They'd say things to me that I would ordinarily say to Roger. They'd talk about my patience or my compassion, and I'd think, "I'm just being Roger." But then I'd hear Roger in my ear saying, "You're just being Chuck."

A decade later, I do not see or talk to Roger much at all. I've moved across the country, and though he's an important part of my past, we do not connect as we once did. Part of growth means being released into the freedom of that new name, that new identity, that new dignity. Roger was a Moses who helped me face and articulate the injustice and pain in my life. He spoke to a deeper dignity and challenged me with a vision for life beyond my brokenness. This very vision required me to leave and become a Moses to others.

As we navigate along this Exodus way in future chapters, you'll see how growth and maturity develops into a life of self-giving that satisfies and fulfills us in ways that far exceed the early days of receiving. The Moses in your life will not engender a slavish devotion or loyalty but challenge you to become a unique image of God. Today one of the great privileges I enjoy is challenging the students I work with to live the particular story God is writing for them. Being a Moses is having a vision for someone that isn't a carbon copy of your own but that allows them to begin to find their own story caught up in God's larger Exodus story.

As we'll see, Moses took some heat along the way, too. Part of the weighty role of being a Moses in someone's life is being able to walk honestly, patiently, and compassionately—even when you'd rather run in the other direction. It's also being willing to see that your own Exodus journey hasn't ended yet. God is continuing to strip you of the chains that constrict your true freedom. Being a Moses is a tough business. And as we'll see in the next chapter, even the biggest victories do not come without a fight.

Discussion

1. What struck you about Jamie's actions in the restaurant? What were some of the features of the story that stood out?

2. What does it mean to take injustice and oppression in your life seriously? How are we all "victims" in one way or another?

3. What is a key message or story or person in your life that keeps you from experiencing a sense of dignity? What would living with greater dignity mean for you?

4. How do you identify with the "broken spirit and cruel slavery" that kept Israel from following Moses? Is there a person in your life who has a vision for more for you?

5. Do you have a desire to become a Moses to someone else? What do you think needs to happen for you to get there?

Chapter 4

Exit Strategy

To let God meet us where we are, we must know where we are, and such an exercise in truth-telling can often be painful.[1]
                                                —Gordon Dalbey

The way of trust is a movement into obscurity, into the undefined, into ambiguity, not into some predetermined, clearly delineated plan for the future. The next step discloses itself only out of a discernment of God acting in the desert of the present moment. The reality of naked trust is the life of the pilgrim who leaves what is nailed down, obvious, and secure, and walks into the unknown without any rational explanation to justify the decision or guarantee the future. Why? Because God has signaled the movement and offered it his presence and his promise.
                                                —Brennan Manning

My first impression of Deanna was hardly positive. I was on the phone with her about her son John, with whom I was just beginning a counseling relationship. She wanted to inject a whole lot of her own thoughts into the process. I listened patiently, secretly hoping it might be our last talk.

It didn't take long before the ragged puzzle pieces of this family began to form a clear picture. In just a few sessions with John, I realized that the entire family was under the oppressive thumb of a cruel tyrant, Deanna's husband. While he took care of his family financially and provided a roof over their heads, he made life inside the home a living hell. After spending several sessions with her son, I realized it was time to bring Deanna in.

A new impression of Deanna soon formed as this woman, short in stature but exuding enough energy for a woman twice her size, walked into the room. She came to that first session ready to talk, and she talked and talked and talked. It was as if years of dammed-up experiences and feelings had burst over the top. Soon the tears began to flow. Deanna hadn't realized that she was in an abusive relationship. It took some time for her to face the truth of her situation, to begin to see her own true dignity and start to own a vision for a life beyond the exhausting oppression she faced each day.

It was time to form an exit strategy from slavery for Deanna. This was not, of course, an exit strategy from her family or even necessarily from her husband. It was an exit strategy designed to pave the way out of the Egypt of abuse she was experiencing. We recognized fully that embracing and speaking the truth was not likely to be received with joy by her husband.

But we knew what we had to do. We set up a meeting with Pharaoh.

Exit Obstacles

Obstacles are a part of every journey. When I married Sara sixteen years ago I was fairly sure, like many young people, that our marriage would be obstacle-free. We enjoyed one another's company, agreed on almost everything, and shared a common vision for a life together. But inevitably we've hit more roadblocks, detours, and dead ends than I ever imagined. There have been times when I wondered if we'd make it. I've learned from married couples much more experienced than we are that it's simply part of the deal. Marriage is a joyful, exhilarating, and treacherous journey. In fact, I'm accepting more and more the painful reality that my heart is so relentlessly committed to its many Egypts that I'll be returning and leaving over and over again for the rest of my life.

Even so, those early pages of the Exodus story disturb me because I want it to be easier. I'd like to skip the grueling roller-coaster ride of Egypt's resistance. I want to see God swoop in on a magic chariot, vanquishing the enemy in an instant and rescuing Israel, his treasured possession. But the story of redemption, which is really the whole story of the Scriptures, is an excruciatingly long, tumultuous narrative full of resistance, battle, defeat, exile, reunion, and rebellion—stretched out over centuries. Couldn't it be simpler somehow?

I still ask myself that question, even after many years of engaging in the thoroughly messy and unpredictable work of pastoring and counseling. Time and again I find myself walking with men and women struggling to break free of their own personal Egypts, searching for a way out and finding obstacle after obstacle in their way. The Exodus teaches us that exit strategies are not very easy at all—and so do the experiences of our own lives.

If I were in charge, Deanna's story would have been much easier. Deanna and I would have made steady progress together until she was ready to sit down and face her husband. At that point, we'd invite him in. He'd be ready to listen attentively to his hurting wife. She would speak honestly and he would affirm her empathetically. He'd own his years of abuse and ask for her forgiveness. We'd agree that healing takes time and he'd respond with understanding and compassion, granting her space to heal. Over time they would build a new trust manifested in renewed commitment and a growing love. We'd end our time together with celebration that I, of course, would continue later with a glass of champagne, toasting to my incredible strategizing. A therapist's dream!

But God's work in our lives was far messier. It turns out that Deanna's husband was not excited to see me—not at all. Our first session together was a disaster. Deanna was not yet ready to confront him with the many years of abuse, exemplified in dozens of stories of dignity-destroying emotional and verbal torment. He, of course, came in ready for a fight. It was easy to see why he didn't trust me—in his eyes, I was the one responsible for throwing a grenade into his family. Suffice it to say, our session became a battle between him and me, with a heartbroken wife and mother watching alongside as her world unraveled.

The Exodus way is paved with roadblocks, detours, and dead ends. Some obstacles—the Pharaohs we live with in an abusive spouse or boss, the external slavery in social or economic struggles—exist outside of us. Yet many obstacles exist within us as well. I didn't recognize that Deanna was not yet ready for that dangerous conversation with her husband. In missing this, I neglected key inner obstacles in her journey out of Egypt.

How do we go about forming an exit strategy in the face of so much resistance? Looking at the whole picture, leaving Egypt seems improbable, if not impossible. Can we even begin to pave a successful path out of slavery given the enormity of the battle?

A Bloody Mess

Deanna's story is unique, but her experience of anguish with an uncertain future rings true to many of us. Crushed under the weight of our circumstances, we begin to wonder if there is any way out. Whether we experience this reality in a dead-end job or through a dark depression or in the midst of a seemingly hopeless battle with infertility, the existential realities feel similar. We feel stuck, trapped, powerless, and perhaps even resigned to the impossibility of change. Life, you might say, feels like a bloody mess.

It is at this moment in Israel's journey that a defining event takes place, marking not only Israel's deliverance but a new identity as a free people. The Passover strikes us, at first, as a gruesome affair, a bloodbath.

> For I will pass through the land of Egypt that night, and I will strike down every firstborn in the land of Egypt, both human beings and animals; on all the gods of Egypt I will execute judgments: I am the LORD. The blood shall be a sign for you on the houses

where you live: when I see the blood, I will pass over you, and no plague shall destroy you when I strike the land of Egypt (Exodus 12:12-13).

To our modern sensibilities, this event seems inhumane, even savage. But I believe it is the key to our exit from slavery.

That original Passover, following the last and most violent of the plagues, signified once and for all that God would not stand for injustice and oppression. A Hallmark card to Pharaoh wouldn't have convinced him to stop his reign of terror. This called for a starker intervention, one that would signify an important reality at the core of the story—that Israel was powerless to overcome its greatest obstacles. A Passover identity acknowledges that life is a bloody mess, overwhelming our own feeble attempts at self-salvation.

That's why God told Israel to remember the Exodus in the Passover feast each year. It was a tangible, embodied way of recollecting the pain of slavery and the sheer graciousness of God's redemption. Describing what happens in the Passover ritual, one rabbi writes, "We taste (in the seder meal) the trauma of slavery in all its bitterness as well as the sweetness of liberation." He continues, "And we realize how fortunate and also how enslaved we are—whether by habits and patterns, relationships that no longer suit us, or memories of the past."[2] In other words, the Passover remembrance cuts to the core of each of our lives with surprising relevance. We cannot fix ourselves.

When the Israelites were told to smear the blood of lambs on the doorposts, God provided them with a new identity.

They were "under the blood," so to speak. Indeed, this was the reality of those most impacted by Pharaoh's terror tactics. But in the ironic economy of redemption, bloodshed covers the Israelites. This blood, however, does not hurt, shame, or further terrorize. In the blood of the lamb, Israel finds liberation, pointing ahead, as it does, to the blood of the true and final Lamb of God, our ultimate liberator.

This redemptive event also points to the heart of Deanna's struggle, as well as our own struggles. Our utter helplessness brings us to the point that we cry for help, confess our utter neediness, and reach out for the hand of our Rescuer.

The Way of Trust

As a therapist, I am armed with a whole host of strategies to help others. In my time with Deanna, we talked about very important practical matters involving boundaries with her husband, financial separation, legal issues, and more. I had her read some of the best literature on emotional abuse and challenged her to join a group for women in similar circumstances. All of this, however, was contingent on a larger reality, a larger need. Deanna and I needed the intervention of a Rescuer.

G. K. Chesterton, the great British writer, once said, "Psychoanalysis is confession without absolution."[3] That's precisely what Christian therapy adds to the relationship. So many people who come for therapy don't realize how much help they really need, how broken they really are. Nothing less than a Passover moment is needed for us to cross into freedom, the honest and vulnerable confession that we cannot overcome our darkest moments without our redeeming, liberating God.

Dietrich Bonhoeffer once commented, "The most experienced psychologist or observer of human nature knows infinitely less of the human heart than the simplest Christian who lives beneath the Cross of Jesus."[4] Bonhoeffer was not trashing therapists; rather, he was putting what we do into perspective. He was reminding us that our strategies are futile apart from the Rescuer's decisive intervention.

Passover is that intervention. As Bonhoeffer suggests, its culmination is in the Cross, where the Lamb was slain for the sake of an ultimate rescue, a once-and-for-all event that marks the ultimate end to slavery and death. Our greatest growth is contingent on this final Passover. It makes possible our exodus from slavery to sin and death in all its familiar forms.

Brian Walsh and Sylvia Keesmaat brilliantly connect the first exodus from slavery with the second exodus in Christ.

> This language of inheritance, forgiveness and rescue from one empire in order to be freed in another kingdom harks back to the exodus narrative. It was Israel who was rescued from the imperial captivity of Egypt. It was Israel who received the promised land as an inheritance. And it was to rebellious Israel that God revealed himself as a God of forgiveness (see Ex. 32:7-34:10). Now, says Paul, we experience an exodus liberation in Jesus. . . . In postmodern terms, this liberation is not in order to enslave us in yet another regime that would violently impose its ideology on us . . . the kingdom of the beloved Son is a kingdom won

not through violence imposed on others but through violence imposed upon the Son.[5]

The blood that is smeared is now the blood of the Lamb, the Son of God, covering you and me and making it possible for us to cross from death to life. You and I cannot experience true freedom without it.

Some find it almost impossible to embrace this reality. So used to self-reliance, we may balk at the notion that we cannot rescue ourselves. Relinquishing control, opening our hearts to a liberator outside ourselves, can fill us with fear. If we've been hurt or wounded in a relationship, it is particularly difficult, perhaps, to imagine a God who will actually show up when we are at the end of our resources. What's more, this God does not invite us into a painless future, a quick fix. The sea crossing leads into desert territory, which, as we will see, holds dangers that require us to remember the Passover again and again. What will we hold on to in these times of trial?

Though God's rescue comes as an unmerited gift, there is a challenge to each of us who dares to engage this story. The apostle Paul writes, "all are now justified freely by his grace through the redemption that came by Christ Jesus. God presented Christ as a sacrifice of atonement, through the shedding of his blood—to be received by faith" (Romans 3:24-25). Only faith, radical trust in a rescuing God, enables us to embrace God's Passover rescue and embark on the wilderness way.

As Brennan Manning points out, this way of trust is anything but easy.

The way of trust is a movement into obscurity, into the undefined, into ambiguity, not into some predetermined, clearly delineated plan for the future. The next step discloses itself only out of a discernment of God acting in the desert of the present moment. The reality of naked trust is the life of the pilgrim who leaves what is nailed down, obvious, and secure, and walks into the unknown without any rational explanation to justify the decision or guarantee the future. Why? Because God has signaled the movement and offered it his presence and his promise.[6]

There are very few guarantees, no matter what exit strategy one chooses. Even the best recipes can disappoint. But there is a strange assurance in Manning's words: "God has signaled the movement and offered it his presence and his promise."

For Deanna, whose husband would refuse to engage any process of counseling that might challenge his position of power, God's "signal" came in and through a series of interesting providences. She began to trust Scripture and to find herself in its story, recognizing that God doesn't want anyone to continue to live in oppressive slavery. In the weekly celebration of the Eucharist she discovered the joy of eating and drinking of the grace of a rescuing Savior. Never before had this liturgical celebration meant so much to her as it did when she discovered its connection to her own exodus. She experienced a deeper connection to God than she had before, relinquishing control more and more as she grew in trust. And she enjoyed a redemptive community, including trusted friends in her support group and good friends who spoke with a common voice. Her "way of trust" was not blind. It was guided by God himself, by Scripture, by acts of participation in God's means of grace, and by community. No longer alone, as she was in Egypt, Deanna would journey into the wilderness with the presence and the promise of God.

We begin our own journey into the wilderness when we honestly admit that life is a bloody mess, when we confess our powerlessness to defeat the enslavements of our lives. It's an exit strategy that defies conventional wisdom and quick fixes. But it's crucial for our successful navigation through the wilderness ahead.

Discussion

1. Why is the way out of Egypt so bloody? How does your life demonstrate how difficult—even bloody—leaving Egypt can be?

2. Why is Passover necessary? What tangible difference does it make for you to admit your own powerlessness and trust the Rescuer?

3. Why is the way of trust both so difficult and so appealing? How is this way different from the way you've lived your life?

Part 2

*

Sinai:
Receiving
Our New
Identity

Chapter 5

The True Story of Your Life

Humanity is in a state of servitude. We frequently do not notice that we are slaves, and sometimes we love it. But humanity also aspires to be set free. It would be a mistake to think that the average person loves freedom. A still greater mistake would be to suppose that freedom is an easy thing. Freedom is a difficult thing.

—Nicolas Berdyaev

"You shall be my treasured possession out of all the peoples. Indeed, the whole earth is mine, but you shall be for me a priestly kingdom and a holy nation."

—Exodus 19:5-6

"Are you born again?"

I was asked this question in a San Francisco coffee shop, and I almost fell out of my chair. Perhaps this guy had noticed my book on Christian spirituality, I thought. It sat next to my laptop, serving as a coaster for my latte.

In an instant it struck me that he might be looking to pick a fight. The question was likely rhetorical bait. I do live in

San Francisco, after all. In South Carolina the same question might be an invitation to a happy testimony-telling time. But I figured this guy had me pegged as a Christian fanatic attempting to invade his safe coffee spot. I was wrong.

He sat down in the chair across from me. In the next hour, he chronicled his journey out of addiction and into faith. This man had clearly spent many years in Egypt. He looked gaunt and pale, and I soon learned that he'd been released from inpatient rehab just a month prior. His older sister lived in San Francisco, and her attic had become his "wilderness" halfway house on the way to recovery. Alone in the big city, he found a few friends in an AA meeting held in the basement of a Baptist church. But this guy was not out of the woods yet.

"I feel real bad, buddy," he said, apologizing for having taken my time. Clearly the self-contempt so pervasive in an addict's heart still plagued him.

He walked out the door like a man headed into a dangerous wilderness, a battlefield of the soul, haunted by his tragic past while fighting the demons ready to rob his future.

Birth Trauma

Israel had enjoyed many good days in the womb of Egypt. They had multiplied and flourished (Exodus 1:7), prospering in ways that brought blessing both to themselves and to Egypt. They became friendly with the locals and enjoyed a good life at the edge of an empire thriving with a wealth and beauty that was the envy of the world. Life was pretty good. But then a new Pharaoh came to town.

Israel was all alone. She was without her God. She'd largely forgotten her noble ancestry in Abraham, Isaac, and

Jacob. And now her good life was lost to the mad manipulations of an evil dictator, an insecure bully who would turn a once-noble people into slaves. Israel had lost her past, and now her present had become precarious. A hopeful future seemed impossible.

Israel's womb had become a tomb.

But God sent a "midwife." Like the midwives who feared God and became protectors to the Israelite children (Exodus 1:17-21), God called Moses to a much more complicated delivery. A man who had been rebirthed himself not long ago would midwife Israel's rebirth as a nation through the waters of the Red Sea.

This rebirth was accompanied by pain and trauma. People left the only homes they'd ever known to enter a wilderness. Many were confused, believing slavery to be preferable to the snakes and scorpions of the vast wilderness of Sinai.

Every moment beyond the sea reminded the Israelites that now they lived in a completely new reality called freedom—but it didn't always feel so free. Like the man who took a seat across from me in a chance encounter at a coffee shop, Israel found that leaving Egypt was not at all easy. Maybe Ezekiel was right: "As for your birth, on the day you were born your navel cord was not cut, nor were you washed with water to cleanse you, nor rubbed with salt, nor wrapped in cloths. No eye pitied you, to do any of these things for you out of compassion for you; but you were thrown out in the open field" (Ezekiel 16:4-5).

Childhood Trauma

I've witnessed two births.

My ten-year-old was delivered by C-section in what seemed, at first, a routine procedure. The problem was, she couldn't breathe. Nurses quickly transported her to intensive care, where she was intubated to assist her breathing.

My eight-year-old's birth was more routine. Like many newborns, she was delivered into her "freedom" with many tears, tears that continued through the ache of colic until she was almost seven months.

My two beautiful daughters entered this world in pain. For every husband who says, "I've never witnessed anything so amazing," I'd agree. But it was also intensely traumatic, for my wife in particular, and for each of my girls in a unique way. In both cases I wondered if my girls might not have wanted to stay a bit longer in the familiar space they'd inhabited for nine months. Yes, they were free from the tight confines of the womb—but for what?

Like a newborn, Israel emerged from the womb with bitter tears at Marah (Exodus 15-16). The great rescue began to feel to them like a cosmic bait-and-switch game that left them unsure if the decision to leave Egypt was the right one after all. Their relief to be free of Pharaoh's grasp turned very quickly to profound dissatisfaction. God had ignited their longing and intensified their hunger for a better life, but the Exodus did not bring the immediate gratification they longed for. Their joy in liberation was tempered by the reality of a long journey through a dry and weary land. Many reminisced about life back in Egypt.

We often talk about being "born again" as if we've left our past behind. But our past comes with us, often haunting us. Freedom's trials can shatter our optimism, making us want to turn back to what was secure and familiar.

I think about the woman I counseled some time ago who was initially so enthusiastic about the new hope she experienced. Ravaged as a child by physical abuse and demeaning comments from her dad, she was just beginning to grasp her own dignity. But then a boyfriend rejected her and she began to doubt her newly forming identity. In this fragile, early stage of therapy, her sense of worth wobbled unsteadily. Late one night, she drank too much at a bar and slept with a stranger. Distraught and hopeless, she called me. "I may as well quit counseling. It's too hard to believe that I'm worth anything. It's probably best to go back to what I'm good at—getting drunk and getting laid."

Her story echoes Israel's story. When Israel emerged from Egypt, she wanted freedom, but she wasn't yet ready for it. Though kept safe in the wilderness by God, she carried the habits and patterns of Egypt in her heart. In the words of the Russian Orthodox theologian Nicolas Berdyaev,

> Humanity is in a state of servitude. We frequently do not notice that we are slaves, and sometimes we love it. But humanity also aspires to be set free. It would be a mistake to think that the average person loves freedom. A still greater mistake would be to suppose that freedom is an easy thing. Freedom is a difficult thing.[1]

This is a different story than the typical evangelical formula for being born again. We're often led to believe that embracing Jesus changes everything, makes you forget your past, and leads you into the "peace that passes all understanding" (Philippians 4:7). We're not often told that once we've been delivered into freedom, the hardest times may still be ahead.

Still, I'm struck by the honesty of the Israelites, an honesty that eludes us at times. After being delivered into freedom, they challenge God and Moses, saying, "If only we had died by the hand of the LORD in the land of Egypt, when we sat by the fleshpots and ate our fill of bread; for you have brought us out into this wilderness to kill this whole assembly with hunger" (Exodus 16:3). They might as well have said, "We miss our old life, our false securities and cheap substitutes. At least they filled our hunger!"

This ancient story teaches us that freedom is truly difficult to embrace. Living into God's liberating story for our life comes at a price. A wilderness awaits. But the wilderness is also where our lives begin to be redefined.

Training Wheels

Like a good parent, God understood that Israel was a frightened child, longing for a little food and drink. After her traumatic delivery, it made sense that she would be frustrated and afraid. At other times in Israel's history God would exercise less patience and more discipline in the face of complaint. But in this moment, just after Israel had been reborn, delivered through the birth waters of the Red Sea and placed in the cold and lonely crib of Marah, God shows understanding.

Like a good parent, God cared for Israel, providing food and drink for her (Exodus 16-17). God had designs on her life. She was to become a queen, beautiful and compelling, giving glory to her God and Lord. But it would take some work to get her there.

Parenting is an incredible privilege, but also a huge and sometimes painful responsibility. When I taught my kids how to ride bikes, I remember running alongside holding both the seat and the handlebars, cheering them on while it felt like my back was breaking. The transition from training wheels to the freedom of confident balance proved excruciatingly delightful.

We started with training wheels. My kids were not yet developmentally ready for the next step. Training wheels were an acknowledgment of this developmental limitation, a necessary step in their journey. Childhood involves limits; kids need boundaries. Don't touch this. Don't go there. Don't eat that. But parents cannot expect complete understanding or compliance because children are children, after all. They don't grasp their own limitations so they disobey, they grumble, they complain. It's the nature of childhood.

Sinai's gift was the law, a set of boundaries to point little children to the way in which they could live and thrive. The apostle Paul calls the law a "tutor"—a teacher for Israel's early days. I've thought of this when I've counseled and pastored people who have recently passed through the waters of the Red Sea. Fresh out of Egypt, we all need some patience along with some clear direction.

Janie needed clear boundaries as she emerged from her own Egypt. She was a helper, an encourager, a person who would be loyal and true no matter what. Immersed in codependency, her Egypt meant being chained to needy people such as her boyfriend, A. J., a hard-charging salesman. A. J. woke up every morning at 6:00 to begin a new day of sales possibilities, returning home late each evening to a doting girlfriend. Although Janie and A. J. had been dating for only two months, already Janie was preparing dinner, doing laundry, and waiting hours past A. J.'s promised arrival. That was what she did best. And that was what A. J. loved about her.

When she began counseling, Janie couldn't imagine anything was wrong. She perceived her behavior as godly and noble. But when her therapist began helping her peel away the layers of enslavement and self-deception, Janie began to recognize her particular attraction to needy, enabling men who took advantage of her need to be needed.

In time, serious about leaving her Egypt of enabling and codependency, she decided to leave A. J. But the patterns of her past life kept intruding on her new path to freedom. Counseling illuminated some of the context for her struggle. Her dad was a narcissistic businessman who'd neglected his family for the pursuit of wealth. Her mom was a children's ministry coordinator at their church, distant and emotionally unavailable to her own children, immersing herself in spiritual things to pacify her own heartache. The oldest of three children, Janie quickly learned that her two brothers were her responsibility. Slavery to the needs of others was ingrained in her earliest years.

This was a painful realization. Janie knew her role. It had become a source of spiritual pride and self-identity. "I can't imagine living any other way," she protested. "You're asking me to disown my only way of loving and serving God."

The counselor responded first by reminding Janie that her desire to serve others was a good thing. This was important for Janie to recognize. It's always important to acknowledge the good desire that stands behind a misdirected way of living. But the counselor continued, "I'm wondering if you might be able to see how your way of loving sabotages relationships, ultimately not allowing others to take responsibility."

It took time for Janie to see this. Leaving Egypt began when Janie left A. J., but it took a lot longer to move out of a lifelong pattern of sacrificing herself at the altar of other people's neediness. Walking slowly and carefully on this new path, each week Jamie and her counselor explored a new facet of this new life of freedom.

This formative time also required some rules, some boundaries. In Janie's case, that meant no dating. This "training wheel" rule could mean the difference between another codependent relationship and learning to walk in freedom. Of course the journey involved more than applying a set of rules. They were part of a life-altering invitation out of one way of living and relating and into another. As Janie followed this basic guidance from her counselor, she found herself beginning to experience more stability and security in herself and in her relationships. The training wheels were working—Janie was learning the joy of riding freely.

Childhood Lessons

If Egypt binds us in a slavery that contradicts God's original design, then the wilderness is about rediscovering that original beauty, dignity, and responsibility. For Israel the first goal of that journey into the wilderness was Sinai. There God reaffirmed his covenant with Israel and gave them the law, through which they could learn what it meant to live and thrive as God's people.

Jewish scholar Jacob Neusner views the law-giving at Sinai as the defining moment in God's great rescue plan. The law, he says, redefines Israel as a people who "accept God's rule and the Torah and all the commandments as the embodiments of that rule."[2] In this new identity as the people of God, Israel would get her dignity back. God's covenant and its corresponding law sets Israel apart as a "treasured possession," a "holy nation," and a "kingdom of priests" (Exodus 19:5-6).

In chapter 1, we found that Israel's story didn't begin with enslavement; it began in Eden, in original beauty and goodness. The Bible roots our core identity in God's original intention for humanity as described in the first two chapters of Genesis. This is the true story of our lives as well.

At Sinai, God sings the lullaby that echoes that original true story. He whispers to his little children, "You are my treasured possession." He speaks words of dignity and glory that an enslaved people long to hear. Sinai represents that moment in each of our lives when it begins to dawn on us that we are more than we seem to be, more than merely ordinary. As we leave our many Egypts throughout the course of our lives, we continually find ourselves at Sinai, the identity checkpoint where we're retold the true story about ourselves.

I experienced such a moment almost fifteen years ago. My world had been turned upside down in seminary. A large piece of my identity had been formed in the Egypt of fear and anxiety, leading me to construct a "false self" around academic performance and competence. This would be the first of many, many Egypts that would be revealed in my life, but it was by far the most earth-shattering to that point. I spent many nights wondering who I was. So much of my "self" was formed to self-protect. I hardly knew how to live differently. But a few Moses-like men and women led me, crawling like a baby, out of Egypt and to Sinai.

As always, I wanted to fast-forward the process. Part of the pull back into Egypt was an attempt to convince myself and others that I'd grown more than they thought. I did not want to be perceived as broken or needy or immature. And for a time, some were convinced that I was growing particularly quickly. But one mentor wasn't so sure. "Chuck, you're like a newborn," he told me one day. "I'd be lying if I told you that you were ready to enter the ministry. You still need some time in the incubator."

I didn't listen. Like Israel, I thought I was far more in control of my life and my emotions than I really was. This mentor was right—I did need more time in the incubator. I needed more time at Sinai, time to look back to where I'd come from, time to consider the new self that was emerging. I needed more time at Sinai discovering that I was God's treasured possession who did not need to perform or succeed for approval. I needed more time drinking in the reality that I was loved and adored by a rescuing and redeeming God.

Identity Re-formation

In our talking GPS culture, we believe that we can always find our way quickly and easily to our desired destination. In a smartphone life, when everything is instantly at our fingertips, we grow impatient when others seem to impede our progress. The cashier at our grocery store takes a bit too much time ringing us up, and we get frustrated. The pastor preaches a little too long, and we feel like precious minutes have been stolen from our Sunday afternoon. We're a busy and anxious people who can't stand waiting.

Our impatience extends to our inner life as well. Someone recently asked, "What's wrong with me that I can't get over the loss of my mother?" She'd lost her mother just a month before and expected the grief to be done. We believe Plato's lie of "mind over matter." Somehow we've duped ourselves into believing that growth and maturity do not require a wilderness; instead we think they can be microwaved, hot and ready.

Sinai stands between Egypt and the Promised Land as a reminder that God is committed to taking as long as you need to form you into the person you were designed to be. "This is your identity. You lost it somewhere along the way. Now let me remind you who you really are."

It's important to remember the first words of the law: "I am the LORD your God, who brought you out of Egypt, out of the land of slavery" (Exodus 20:2). With that preamble, what follows is a charter of freedom, a way of living that fits a people who are loved and redeemed by their creator God.

In that context, the Ten Commandments are not merely restrictions but invitations to a flourishing life. In defining our relationship with God and with each other, the Ten Commandments set up the boundaries in which we may freely live. Each one of the commandments either fences off enslavement or embodies holy liberty.

When my mentor told me that I needed more time in the incubator, he was telling me that training wheels would be necessary for a time. I needed to return to the basics. I needed to be under the care of a Moses, someone who had walked further. I needed to grieve old patterns of living and own how my false identities had hurt others. I needed to grow in my desire for a better life lived out of a new identity in God. In other words, I needed to let go of that need to control that I learned in Egypt and allow God to teach me the true story of my identity.

But I also needed to begin listening. Amidst the voices in my life competing for attention and allegiance was a new voice, the voice of a God who wanted me to know that I was treasured, loved, worth pursuing. A new relationship was forming that didn't require perfection on my part but invited participation in God's new family and God's grand story. But it would take years for that voice to break through the others.

It turns out that being born again isn't easy. Most of us will be invited out of slavery and into a wilderness. Though the days can be long, the God of Sinai is in relentless pursuit—the God who reminds you that you've been rescued, the God who casts a vision for your flourishing, the God whose wise parenting will get you through the rough terrain ahead.

Discussion

1. Why is being delivered out of Egypt so traumatic at times? How has it been traumatic or difficult for you?

2. How does Egypt cause us to lose our identity? How have the Egypts in your life clouded your sense of identity in God?

3. How does God begin to piece together our identity again? How do you feel about this process?

4. How does knowing that you are called a "treasured possession" make a difference? How do you feel when you hear the words of dignity God speaks over you?

5. Think about a particular Egypt in your own life. Now consider how God wants you to both enjoy the good desire for it and also grieve its enslavement of you. Take some time to reflect and write about how God is inviting you to the true story of your life and identity.

Chapter 6

The Real Mission of Your Life

L et us not underestimate how hard it is to be compassionate. Compassion is hard because it requires the inner disposition to go with others to the place where they are weak, vulnerable, lonely, and broken. But this is not our spontaneous response to suffering. What we desire most is to do away with suffering by fleeing from it or finding a quick cure for it. —Henri Nouwen

We do not exist for ourselves alone, and it is only when we are fully convinced of this fact that we begin to love ourselves properly and thus also love others. What do I mean by loving ourselves properly? I mean, first of all, desiring to live, accepting life as a very great gift and a great good, not because of what it gives us, but because of what it enables us to give to others.

—Thomas Merton

✳✳✳

For generations, every little Jewish boy and girl memorized one biblical phrase that encapsulated their faith, the *shema*: "Hear, O Israel: The LORD is our God, the LORD alone. You shall love the Lord your God with all your heart, and with all your soul, and with all your might. Keep these words that I am commanding you today in your heart" (Deuteronomy 6:4-5).

This keystone of Israel's faith unites two essential aspects of faith: loving God and keeping God's commandments. Jesus draws on that passage in responding to a direct question from the religious leaders of his day who ask him to name the greatest command in all of Scripture. "'You shall love the Lord your God with all your heart, and with all your soul, and with all your mind.' This is the greatest and first commandment. And a second is like it: 'You shall love your neighbor as yourself.' On these two commandments hang all the law and the prophets'" (Matthew 22:37-40).

Quoting from both Deuteronomy and Leviticus, Jesus sums up God's commandments in one word: *love*. Love and law are not polar opposites but two aspects of our relationship with God. Keeping God's commandments is not an act of sheer obedience, much less a means by which we earn God's favor. We keep God's commandments because we love him. As Jesus put it: "If you keep my commandments, you will abide in my love, just as I have kept my Father's commandments and abide in his love" (John 15:10).

Knowing that legalistic slavery erodes our dignity and twists our identity, Jesus directs us back to the very heartbeat of Sinai's law—love. Because Jesus sees us as an orphaned and abused people in need of love, he pursues our hearts with a fierceness that renews, restores, and revives our capacity for it.

Now God's beloved Son invites you to identify the places in your life where love's flame has been dimmed or destroyed so that he can rekindle it once again.

Love's Wound

If the Israelites learned anything in Egypt, it was not love but survival. They were no longer in their homeland, Canaan, and the stories they told one another about the old days of Abraham, Isaac, and Jacob might well have portrayed a distant, primitive past. The Israelites had not only survived but flourished in Egypt for more than 400 years (see Exodus 1:7).

Then suddenly things took a turn for the worse. A new Pharaoh used and abused the last generation of Israelites in Egypt. Even in their liberation, they experienced trauma in leaving "home," following an upstart leader who promised freedom. Think about this for a moment, because it reveals another side of this great story.

Could the Israelites trust Moses? Perhaps he had experienced a falling-out with Pharaoh and was using God-talk to manipulate them into following him, wreaking economic havoc on the empire. Or perhaps Moses was simply delusional and sadistic, seeing things that made sense to him but would only bring harm and destruction to his people. How could the Israelites be sure of this grand scheme and its schemer?

From every angle, Israel faced dangerous realities. They might have been slaves, but at least they had homes to live in and food to eat. The land of slavery felt like home, while the vast wilderness was a foreign and hostile environment. What was once sure no longer seemed sure. Being at home in slavery seemed better to them than wandering the wilderness in freedom. In a moment like this, who can you trust? Israel must have wanted to believe and be free and at the same time must have doubted almost everything she was hearing.

Perhaps you've experienced moments like this in your life, moments in which you heard the words of a supposed friend with suspicion, or a risk you took seemed ludicrous after the fact, or cynicism and fear slowly eroded a faint glimmer of hope.

Thrust into the wilderness without adequate food or shelter, Moses tells the Israelites to trust God, remembering once again the story of their rescue and believing that this distant covenant God is trustworthy.

If I'd been one of those Israelites wandering in the wilderness, I might have been hesitant too. With hindsight, we think we would have obeyed so much better than they did—not complaining, not demanding, not losing hope or doubting love. But let's be honest. Pledging to love and follow God would not have come easy, given all that had happened.

Life's painful twists and turns often erode our sense of trust and hope and even lead us to despair. As I write this, the suicide of Bill Zeller, a promising young computer science student at Princeton, is being widely reported and discussed. Most suicides do not make national news, but Zeller left a four-thousand-word note on his website articulating the pain of betrayal with its inevitable emotional fallout. He began by recounting a tragic childhood: "My first memories as a child are of being raped, repeatedly. This has affected every aspect of my life. This darkness, which is the only way I can describe it, has followed me like a fog, but at times intensified and overwhelmed me."

Describing the dramatic impact of the abuse on his everyday life, he noted that he felt trapped in a contaminated body that no amount of washing could clean. Forced to cope with the demands of life, he binged on work. He exercised tirelessly. He drank compulsively. He fought insomnia and exhaustion. He did anything and everything he could to eradicate the feeling of dis-ease, to no avail.

Of Zeller's many wounds, the most painful was the relational wound. Though he sought to cope in a myriad of ways, he simply could not dull the pain or overcome what I would call "love's wound," the deepest blow to his soul. In his attempts to find love, he was faced again and again with slavery's memories. "But as we got closer emotionally," he wrote, "the darkness would return, and every night it'd be me, her and the darkness in a black and gruesome threesome. He would surround me and penetrate me and the more we did the more intense it became. . . . Relationships didn't work. . . . I know now that the darkness will never leave."

How does one man's suicide make national news? Zeller was not merely a promising young Princeton student. Rather, Zeller's *story* made the news. His tragedy, with which so many could identify, made the news. His many ways of coping made the news. And in the end, his relational hopelessness made the news, as it connected with the brokenness so many people experience each day.

The defining betrayal of abuse in Zeller's childhood marked the rest of his life. His Egypt experience evolved into twisted ways of coping through food and alcohol. But the greatest tragedy of all was the relational fallout. He wanted to love but could not do it. He wanted to live but could not muster the strength. The imprint of Egypt was just too intense.

Egypt erodes our ability to will something better for our lives. It stifles our capacity for freedom. Perhaps more than anything else, it squelches our God-given gift to love. Perhaps this is why love occupies the central place in God's commandments. God knows that we're hurt; God knows that we need to be wooed back into a trusting relationship in the midst of our pain.

This is the central message of the book of Hosea, written many years after the Exodus—a time when Israel had rebelled, losing themselves again in idol worship, false loves, murder, and much more, forgetting their covenant God. But Hosea woos them by retelling the love story of the Exodus, when God met Israel in her pain and won her heart. "Therefore I will now allure her, and bring her into the wilderness, and speak tenderly to her. From there I will give her her vineyards, and make the Valley of Achor a door of hope. There she shall respond as in the days of her youth, as at the time when she came out of the land of Egypt" (Hosea 2:14-15). Hosea calls the Exodus time "the days of her youth"—the days of childhood when her capacity for love would be either matured or lost.

When I read Zeller's honest and moving suicide note, I saw a man whose capacity to love had been shattered. Clearly he wanted to love. But in risking love, he found only greater despair. Eventually he could not believe that anything other than darkness would define him.

Dan Allender expresses this paradox of love: "Love may be necessary for survival but daily existence seems to make love impossible. Love is essential, but it seems maddeningly unreasonable. It is both what we desire and despise, wait for and ignore, work toward and sabotage."[1] Bill Zeller worked toward love, perhaps with greater determination than most.

Yet the quest for love brought him more pain than anything else. Ultimately he feared being alone more than he feared death.

Love's Cure

As a clinical intern, one of my first clients was a man twice my age. His first question to me was "How young are you?" Only twenty-seven at the time, I was already feeling completely inadequate. This was not a promising start. But he decided to give me a chance.

Two or three sessions in, we began talking about his father, not an uncommon place to start. I've never met a client who wasn't disappointed in some way or another with a parent or caregiver. Now the father of eight- and ten-year-olds, I've contributed to the grand story of parental disappointment myself. As my client talked more, it became clear that one particular part of his relationship with his father haunted him more than any other.

"My dad and I never played catch," he said. "He was always too busy. Sometimes I'd leave my glove in a conspicuous place, like on his desk. I'd hope he might see it and get the message."

As he reflected on this, something shifted in our relationship with one another. He began asking me big questions. Is this normal? Am I crazy to feel this way? Do you understand how hurt I am? Despite our quarter-century age difference, he was starting to trust me to guide him through his confusion.

In our first sessions, he'd often come in a bit late, but then I noticed that he began arriving early, anxious to get started. He was much more relaxed. He stopped posturing. He no longer reminded me that he had a son my age. "I feel like you're the first man I've ever been able to relate to," my client said one day, looking at me for a reaction. Would I laugh? Would I dismiss him? Might I reject him? Later that night I asked my clinical supervisor about this interaction. My supervisor said, "You're becoming his father." Puzzled, I decided to simply continue being a loving, compassionate presence during our sessions.

One evening during the baseball playoffs, we began our session by talking about the possibility of the Yankees winning their second World Series in three years. My client recalled the years of DiMaggio, Mantle, and Maris, the glory days of the Yankees—a time when every little boy wanted to grow up to be a Yankee. "Chuck, all I wanted was for him to throw me ground balls and fly balls," he said, looking down at the carpet and squeezing his hands together so tightly that I could see the blood constricting in his fingers. "Why wouldn't he play with me?"

"I don't know why," I told my client, leaning in toward him. He was still looking at the floor. I asked him to look at me for a moment. Reluctantly, he raised his eyes, which were already full of tears. I said, "I know this. I've come to enjoy these times with you more than you know. And I'd love to play catch with you."

The dam broke, and tears flowed in a torrent. It was one of the most stunning, sacred moments of my life. Before me sat a man who was twice my age and yet a little boy, an influential businessman but a rejected child.

In an instant, I discovered the power of relationship.

Scripture calls this covenant love.

Love's Centrality

God is a covenant-maker. God operates out of a kind of marital bond in which two parties vow love and faithfulness, in much the same way couples do at their wedding. Over and over God declares: "I will take you as my people, and I will be your God" (Exodus 6:7).

The intimacy of these words, with which God sets the tone for Israel's life and mission, displays the heartbeat of a God who will not settle for mere behavioral conformity or heartless obedience. Everything would be recentered around relationship, and love would define God's relationship with Israel.

The people God embraces in a covenant relationship are enslaved, broken, bruised, and battered. These are not the "who's who" or the cream of the crop. They may be nobodies, but they are not unknown. God has not forgotten them. God will not leave them nor forsake them. God will show endless compassion toward them.

Compassionate love is, indeed, a difficult thing. As Henri Nouwen writes:

Compassion is hard because it requires the inner disposition to go with others to the place where they are weak, vulnerable, lonely, and broken. But this is not our spontaneous response to suffering. What we desire most is to do away with suffering by fleeing from it or finding a quick cure for it. . . . And so we ignore our greatest gift, which is our ability to enter into solidarity with those who suffer. Those who can sit in silence with their fellow man, not knowing what to say but knowing that they should be there, can bring new life in a dying heart. Those who are not afraid to hold a hand in gratitude, to shed tears in grief and to let a sigh of distress arise straight from the heart can break through paralyzing boundaries and witness the birth of a new fellowship, the fellowship of the broken.[2]

Because of our brokenness, God demonstrates love by coming near. God embodies covenant love in his enduring faithfulness, in his unwillingness to be deterred by our ugliness. Though we may despair even to the point of suicide, God is endlessly hopeful, relentlessly loving, despite our own feelings of being unlovable.

Finally, God's covenant love breaks through even the impassable barrier between the divine and the human. God becomes Love in Jesus. "The Word became flesh and blood, and moved into the neighborhood. We saw the glory with our own eyes, the one-of-a-kind glory, like Father, like Son, Generous inside and out, true from start to finish" (John 1:14, *The Message*).

This "boots on the ground" love, this inexorable covenant pursuit, is the only thing in the world that has the capacity to renew our lives but also has the capacity to ignite our hearts with compassionate love toward others. Nothing is more effective in stirring our hearts to love as experiencing it firsthand.

We have the extraordinary task of being living illustrations of God's love today. In that sacred moment with a client twice my age, I discovered something more powerful than theological answers or psychological techniques. It's when we "move into the neighborhood" with compassion for another that real transformation takes place.

To love in this way means "courageously setting aside our personal agenda to move humbly into the world of others with their well-being in view, willing to risk further pain in our souls, in order to be an aroma of life to some and an aroma of death to others."[3] It means, at some level, seeing ourselves caught up in Jesus' vocation of self-sacrificial love. Christ's incarnation now defines the shape of the Christian mission. It is not merely to preach Christ, but to *be* Christ to others.

Thomas Merton writes, "We do not exist for ourselves alone, and it is only when we are fully convinced of this fact that we begin to love ourselves properly and thus also love others. What do I mean by loving ourselves properly? I mean, first of all, desiring to live, accepting life as a very great gift and a great good, not because of what it gives us, but because of what it enables us to give to others."[4] While Egypt erodes our desire to live and love, Sinai's covenant of love begins to reclaim it, restoring the wonder of love, inviting us to trust God for the sake of restoring a broken world, and challenging us to love ourselves, and in so doing, love others.

Bill Zeller took his life, in large part, because an abuser took it from him many years earlier. The good news is that God does not require us to dig our own way out of Egypt. God is the great Lover who meets us in the wilderness in order to win our hearts back. Much happens in our lives that creates distrust, cynicism, bitterness, shame, and fear. However, if you're up for the journey, God wants to rescue you— not just from your slavery but for a life of love.

Discussion

1. How has Egypt eroded your ability to trust others?

2. What relational patterns that have emerged from your past slavery can you identify?

3. How does God's invitation to love challenge you? What are the biggest obstacles?

4. Think about the "Egypts" in your life. In what way do you struggle with believing that God wants to move toward you in your slavery? What evidence can you find that God cares?

Chapter 7

The Futility of Figuring It Out

The real trap, however, is self-rejection. As soon as someone accuses me or criticizes me, as soon as I am rejected, left alone, or abandoned, I find myself thinking, "Well, that proves once again that I am a nobody." My dark side says I am no good. . . . I deserve to be pushed aside, forgotten, rejected, and abandoned. Self-rejection is the greatest enemy of the spiritual life because it contradicts the sacred voice that calls us the "Beloved." Being the Beloved constitutes the core truth of our existence.

—Henri Nouwen

No matter how much grace God has blessed us with, we forever remain dependent on its continuing flow.

—Gerald May

✳✳✳

My father might be called a pack rat. I've asked why he'd keep old pocket watches and random pictures of people we cannot identify and a 1980s Hammond organ that might net $25 in a yard sale. "I feel connected to certain moments from our past through them," he says.

Sit down with my father and he'll tell you stories, recalling obscure moments the rest of us have long forgotten. His nostalgic moments are endearing and his stories fascinating. Even though his pack rat habits are sometimes annoying, all of us who love him get it. These things connect him to times that held special importance. They connect him to the past and bring the past into the present.

When leaving Egypt, the Israelites were not able to hire moving companies to transport their belongings. What accompanied them were memories. Having spent centuries in Egypt, habits and patterns were formed, memories made, traditions solidified. Unlike my dad, the Israelites had few possessions to remind them of the past. Nevertheless, their minds and hearts held what their hands couldn't hold. Only a few weeks into their sojourn, the smells, the scents, and the securities of Egypt haunted them, despite the prospect of a new hope and a new land. We can only speculate on the many fireside conversations beginning with "Do you remember when . . . ?"

Perhaps you can relate. Maybe you find yourself in conversations that start with "Do you remember when . . . ?" Are there places or events that hold significant meaning in your life, memories that haunt you and even seem to plead with you to return?

We cannot underestimate how difficult it must have been for the Israelites to venture forward in this journey, trusting in God. Their difficulties have much to show us about our own journey, and their ways of coping are all too familiar to restless souls like ours.

Restless Waiting

I can understand how the Israelites fell so quickly into idolatry not forty days into their wilderness journey—and so can you. Insecurity and uncertainty frustrate us. The anxious feeling that wells up in moments like these sends us running for our old habits. Irritation and anger grow. A feeling of entitlement whispers, "You deserve more." I know this all too well, and I've worked with enough people to know that these inner mechanisms are universal. We are the Israelites of old, and our security strategies are not so different from theirs.

Imagine for a moment that you are camped at the base of Sinai. You've left the only home you've ever known. The comforts of city living are now just a memory. You cannot walk to the market to buy fruit or visit a neighbor for some bread. The taste of sand in your mouth leaves you thirsty, and the mysterious manna doesn't eradicate the deeper hunger for an answer to your many questions about the future, let alone the very uncertain present.

Finally, a word. Moses says that guidance is coming: God will speak.

Soon enough, Moses returns with God's directives (Exodus 20-23). The Ten Commandments spell out what the good life entails. In order to flourish and to progress in their journey, Israel needs to embrace God's navigation instructions. The law reveals God's original design for Israel as human beings made in and for relationship. The words are dramatic and convicting, and the focus is on the importance of relationship—relationship with God, with parents, with neighbors, with animals, with slaves, with foreigners. Hearing them, you can't help but feel as if God knows your heart! God's words pierce to the core. Some people are blushing as God's directives expose misguided ways of treating others, selfish motives, and arrogant agendas. God's radical new social and relational norms become the talk of the community. To top it off, God addresses your big anxiety about the future. An angel will go before Israel, clearing the way for a successful journey to the promised land.

Along with your fellow sojourners you proclaim, "All that you have spoken we will do." The memories of Egypt fade as your heart surges with hope for a better future.

Then Moses disappears into the clouds again, this time for forty days and forty nights. At this point you're becoming anxious, angry, perplexed. Forty days and forty nights! It feels like an eternity. "Is Moses dead?" someone asks. "But he was our only connection to God," another replies. "Maybe he's given up on us," says still another.

These are human reactions. We cannot be quick to judge them.

You see, as we read the Exodus account, we've got to feel the flow of the story and experience the people's emotions. We've got to place ourselves in its gripping and personal narrative. We cannot fall victim to a kind of chronological arrogance, assuming that we, as modern enlightened people, would react and respond differently.

Sense the urgency the Israelites must have felt as they waited, day after day, for forty days and forty nights, for a word from God. Identify with the restlessness they must have experienced camping in the desert far away from all modern Egyptian conveniences and satisfactions, with little sense of when the waiting would end. Can you blame them for clamoring for the securities of Egypt? Can you imagine the ache they'd feel in the midst of this extended absence?

Coping with God's Absence

I still have the stuffed animal my father gave me when I was born. It's a little lamb, and it has traveled far and wide with me. As a child I called it "Lamby." It accompanied me on every sleepover in my early years. It even traveled to college with me. Today it sits in a box near my bed, rarely exposed to the light of day but too precious to give up.

Psychologists call these things transitional objects. Our favorite childhood stuffed animal, blanket, or doll allows us to make the transition from close proximity to Mom to sleeping in our own beds. It creates a sense of security. And its loss in our early years can be traumatic. I remember misplacing our daughter's security blanket once when she was very young. Nothing could replace it. Her tears compelled us to search high and low until we found it—and only then could she relax.

When the Israelites left Egypt, they left behind much of what gave them security. But they had Moses. While God showed up in signs and wonders, Moses was a steady, embodied presence, perhaps serving as a kind of security blanket for a fearful Israel. In one sense, Moses was God-in-the-flesh, the earthly embodiment of God's presence. Moses could be heard, touched, even argued with. And so when Moses disappeared for forty days, so did Israel's sense of security. After weeks of waiting, the Israelites went to Aaron, Moses' second-in-command, saying, "Come, make gods for us; as for this fellow Moses who brought us up out of Egypt, we don't know what has happened to him" (Exodus 32:1, NIV).[1] Like angry and despairing children who have lost their security blankets, the Israelites were distraught.

Israel did what she knew how to do. In Moses' absence she crafted something to be the presence of God she so desperately longed for. Gathering the gold earrings of men, women, and children acquired in Egypt, Aaron crafted for his people a golden calf, saying, "These are your gods, O Israel, who brought you up out of the land of Egypt!" (Exodus 32:4). It's as if the Israelites were saying, "We need something we can touch, something we can see, something we can pray to." If we're honest, we can relate to that desire too.

Our idols are touchstones of the transcendent. They give us a sense of control, of access, of intimacy and connection. It would be easy to point the finger at Israel if we didn't have a hundred different ways of manufacturing a sense of security in our own lives. We've got shopping therapy or chocolate therapy. We find the transcendent in a bottle of wine or in a moment of false intimacy through pornography. We seek security in wealth, in academic credentials, in reputation. When left unsatisfied, our longing for the transcendent leads to a frantic search for a more expedient way. We long for something we can touch, taste, see—and control.

And let's face it, expediency has become epidemic. I find myself easily irritated when I have to wait, whether it's in traffic or at a stoplight or in a line at the grocery store. I'm frustrated by a YouTube video buffering, or when my cable goes out, or when there's no ATM nearby, or when my wife doesn't quickly return a phone call. North American culture has institutionalized expediency. The quick and efficient has become an entitlement. As a therapist, many of the struggles I see playing out in people's lives can be summed up as a failure to wait, to long, to grieve in the midst of the delay.

The Exodus story is predicated on waiting, and the Exodus story is our story too. It is the Christian story. We wait on a God who says, "Just a little while longer . . ." And we're waiting not just for God to return, but we wait in the midst of extraordinary difficulties. Ask a woman who is infertile to "wait a little longer" or to "trust a bit more" and you'll witness an appropriate sense of injustice and rage. Ask someone who has cancer to be patient with God for a cure and you may get an angry glare. Tell a victim of abuse that healing will take a long time and she'll likely recoil with self-defeat and despair. In the midst of our pain, the small satisfaction of a golden calf often feels better than seemingly endless waiting.

Where Is God?

In the chapters of Exodus that follow the incident of the golden calf (25-31), God is busy—very busy. While the Israelites wait in uncertainty, God is busy giving Moses detailed instructions about the tabernacle. Why? Because the tabernacle was the place where God would once again renew relationship with Israel. The tabernacle would become the centerpiece of God's restoration project, the very dwelling place of God among God's people. So while the people waited, God was actively pursuing an agenda of restoration.

Where is God? The first disciples may have wondered that too as they heard Jesus talking about leaving them. Yet as Jesus prepares them for his death, he tells them he is going ahead to prepare a place for them . . . in fact, he'll be taking up residence in their hearts by his Spirit (John 14:2, 17). The apostle Paul explains that the body is God's temple (1 Corinthians 6:19), and John casts a vision of a city where God will dwell permanently in a new heaven and a new earth (Revelation 21). Where is God? God was busy back then, with Moses. And God is busy now. God is not Aristotle's Unmoved Mover; he's a Mover. He's building. He's preparing. But let's be honest. The delay is frustrating, even maddening at times.

Where is God? When we're not sure, we look in odd places—in the energy surge of a shopping binge, in the thrill of high stakes poker. Of course, God is not really there. What is there is a feeling of the transcendent, a dopamine surge of glory that elevates us beyond our momentary pain. It's the illusive feeling of control—even if only for a brief time. It's a golden calf taste of Egypt's old securities.

During the reign of King Hezekiah, the threat of invasion sent the king scrambling for help. In a moment of desperation, Hezekiah sends envoys to Egypt, reversing the Exodus journey, to beg for help. In response, the Lord declares, "Woe to the obstinate children . . . to those who carry out plans that are not mine, forming an alliance, but not by my Spirit, heaping sin upon sin; who go down to Egypt without consulting me; who look for help to Pharaoh's protection, to Egypt's shade for refuge" (Isaiah 30:1-2, NIV).

The phrase "Egypt's shade" is telling. We could just as well substitute in its place "Egypt's security blanket." It's as if God is saying, "Hezekiah, you're a good king; why would you go back to childhood habits when you're all grown up?" The alliance Hezekiah seeks may well bring him temporary safety, but it is bound to be an epic failure. No good can come from reversing the Exodus. Egypt's securities are mere illusions.

It's no surprise that we go back to our old security strategies in the midst of God's apparent absence, whether in work or sport or less acceptable addictions like drugs or porn. We are searching for something that can assure us. In a sense, our golden calves assume a kind of personality that speaks to us: "Come to me and I'll hold you for a bit. I know you're scared." Surely we can relate to the Israelites as they grasp for control.

Where was God? In a blend of irony, tragedy, and even a bit of comedy, while the Israelites were desperately crafting their substitute God-presence, God was busy making plans to be more present with them than ever. And while we're desperately seeking our own substitutes for security, God's Son, as the carpenter he was raised to be, is building a home for his restless and weary pilgrim children.

Self-Destruction

Egypt's tug is confusing. As we've seen in previous chapters, Israel's early days in Egypt were magical. Egypt was a refuge in a time of famine, a safe haven for a people who needed a sense of security and permanency. Our idols and addictions often begin in the same way—with a good desire. No one picks up a drink in order to become an alcoholic or a donut in order to develop an eating disorder. Our desires are so often twisted and God's original design so often distorted that we forget the original plan.

In God's seeming absence, we forget that we are God's treasured possession. We forget that God has been busy redeeming and restoring. Or perhaps our memory betrays us, convincing us that Egypt was a better fit, that slavery held better opportunity.

But the slavery of Egypt destroys our God-given dignity. It erodes hope and causes us to forget God's loving pursuit. Instead we craft ways of self-sabotage. We turn to idols and addictions that violate God's intention for us and damage us in both soul and body. Henri Nouwen describes this strange phenomenon:

> The real trap, however, is self-rejection. As soon as . . . I am rejected, left alone, or abandoned, I find myself thinking, "Well, that proves once again that I am a nobody." My dark side says I am no good . . . I deserve to be pushed aside, forgotten, rejected, and abandoned. Self-rejection is the greatest enemy of the spiritual life because it contradicts the sacred voice that calls us the "Beloved." Being the Beloved constitutes the core truth of our existence.[2]

Idolatry is, in fact, a form of self-rejection. It is human self-sabotage, a rejection of our dignity and a rejection of the One who bestows it. It is bigger than our destructive habits and patterns because at its core it annihilates *us,* destroying our capacity to love, to trust, to hope. It is a slow erosion process. It begins, perhaps, with a golden calf, but it ends in devastation of mind, body, and spirit.

In those forty days and nights, Israel forgot that she was the Beloved. And it was eating away at her, quite literally. The "self-rejection" Nouwen describes amounts to a denial that we are God's imagebearers, a rejection of our original design and our ultimate satisfaction. But when we are crafting our golden calves, this reality is far from our thoughts.

I received a Facebook invitation recently from someone I hadn't heard from in many, many years—since elementary school. The image I had of this person was of a bright, shining star, a young and successful person who impressed me, impressed my parents, and seemed destined for good things. When I saw his Facebook picture, I was struck by how poorly he had aged. A mutual friend told me that this new Facebook friend had unsuccessfully battled alcoholism for decades. This once-successful man had lost good jobs, experienced multiple divorces, and seen his body turn on him. At fifty-three, he looked like a man in his seventies.

Idolatry devastates God's design, not merely for creation but for us. We become what we despise. It happens slowly, almost invisibly. But it happens. A workaholic loses his family despite significant financial gain. A relationship addict finds herself experiencing yet another betrayal. After twenty-five years a pastor's wife leaves her husband, a shell of a man despite his many ministry successes. Golden calves look shiny at first, but their greatest damage is done in time, rotting us from the inside out.

Relentless Pursuit

It's tempting to conclude that our own golden calves are bad, and that we should avoid them at all costs. We think, perhaps, that we can muster up enough energy to fight off the temptation, to relinquish control, to avoid Israel's fatal mistake. But idolatry and addiction are more subtle and crafty than that.

Because many of our idols and addictions are twisted forms of the good things God created, they entice us into believing that they will bring us the security, comfort, and control we need. Mere willpower is not enough to counter the subtle tug of a sight, a sound, or a smell of something we really love and want.

Why isn't willpower enough? Consider that our minds and bodies are extraordinarily complex creations. The best science on addiction today reminds us that Israel had little chance to combat the deeply ingrained patterns and habits learned in Egypt. Neural pathways had been formed during the years of slavery to such an extent that, says addiction expert and psychiatrist Gerald May, "The brain does not forget." He writes,

> From the standpoint of psychology, we can never become so well-adjusted that we can stop being vigilant. From a neurological viewpoint, it means the cells of our best-intentioned systems can never eradicate the countless other systems that have been addicted. And from a spiritual perspective, it means that no matter how much grace God has blessed us with, we forever remain dependent on its continuing flow.[3]

It doesn't take an addiction expert to convince us of humankind's basic selfishness. We are prone to self-protection, and it is often difficult to combat this primal urge to control, to react, to protect rather than to risk, to trust, to believe. Israel was doing what came naturally to her—attempting to bring some order into her chaos.

Of course this does not mean we can abdicate our responsibility. But it does help to understand why our wilderness battles with idolatry and addiction can be so profoundly difficult. Simple willpower is not enough. Self-help strategies may help for a time but will ultimately fail. What we need is bigger than us. What we need is love.

God's relentless pursuit of us in the midst of our many returns to Egypt is stunning. In the midst of our shame and guilt, it's hard to believe that God has any intention of returning to restore us and even rebuild relationship with us. We live in a world that makes us pay when we screw up. Even when others extend grace to us, it feels as if we have to do something—anything—to fix the problem. We are chronic self-fixers.

Amazingly, God continues to reach out to the rebellious Israelites with relentless love and grace—"keeping steadfast love for the thousandth generation, forgiving iniquity and transgression and sin" (Exodus 34:7). This love is not merely the behavior of a reluctant friend. Instead it reflects God's *character*—God is "merciful and gracious, slow to anger, and abounding in love and faithfulness" (v. 6). It's amazing because this is so unusual, both in our everyday lives and in our understanding of the God of the Bible.

God's focus is not just forgiveness but restoration. God's tabernacle plans would go on, as nothing less than God's abiding presence would ultimately comfort the fearful hearts of the people. To his wary disciples, Jesus promised that a Comforter and an Advocate would come, the Spirit of truth, entering the very hearts of God's people in order to take up residence forever (John 14:16-17). In other words, God would tabernacle more closely than ever, dwelling in us, advocating for us, comforting us in the midst of our pain. Jesus knew that nothing less than God's relentless love could cure our weary and fearful souls.

To be sure, until Jesus returns, the old memories of Egypt will haunt us. Our continuing battle with golden calves reminds us that we're continually seeking a kind of satisfaction that we can bottle up, box in, possess. Most of us are pack rats, after all. We're not fond of letting go, of surrendering, of embracing a new way.

But as we'll see, God continues to pursue us on this wilderness journey with a love that strips away our old selves and energizes our new and better selves. In time we'll learn to relax, to relinquish control, to receive the love God wants to give us. In time. Meanwhile, waiting is so difficult.

Discussion

1. What do the golden calves in our lives signify? What are we really longing for?

2. Think of some ways in which you grasp for control. In what sense might this grasping be seen as a longing for God?

3. What emotions arise as you place yourself in the Exodus story, waiting for the return of Moses? Do you experience anger, regret, sadness, abandonment, loss? How do some of these feelings play out as you wait on God today?

4. In the midst of God's seeming absence, he is really quite busy. How does knowing that God continues to pursue you encourage you in difficult times?

Chapter 8

Disobedient Obedience

A brother in Scetis committed a fault. A council was called to which Moses was invited, but he refused to go to it. Then the priest sent someone to him, saying, "Come, for everyone is waiting for you." So he got up and went. He took a sack, filled it with sand and cut a small hole at the bottom and carried it on his shoulders. The others came out to meet him and said, "What is this, father?" The Abba said to them, "My sins run out behind me, and I do not see them, and today I am coming to judge the errors of another." When they heard that, they said no more to the brother but forgave him.

—Desert Fathers

Sinai, not Egypt, is Israel's largest roadblock to Canaan.

—Stephen Dempster

✳✳✳

Living in San Francisco gives me the opportunity to have regular conversations with skeptics, people who like much of what they see in Jesus but who dislike Christians. Just recently a friend asked, "Why can't Christians have fun?"

My friend went on to talk about the "stuffy" church his parents occasionally went to. His perception of the Christian faith was that it's "all about duties and rules and nos." He talked about his Christian friends being "repressed" and "robotic." I understood—some of that may be true. But then he went on to say, "I hate that the Old Testament is all about rules and commands. I like Jesus because he's all about love."

My friend's analysis may appear to be true from a distance, but it misses the point. I'm convinced that finding God in the wilderness requires us to see God's law as a life-giving guide for living out our new identity as God's covenant people, not as a life-sucking burden.

The Law That Divides

I remember Jace as a hard-working, successful Christian businessman who was a leader in his church and in the community. So I was surprised when a mutual friend told me about Jace's double life, hiding a longtime battle with alcoholism. After a DUI, his wife began to reach out for help among their friends, and Jace finally woke up. He came clean, entered a rehab facility, and got sober.

At some level, this split between public persona and private reality is true for all of us. Parts of us are better left undisclosed; our secret thoughts are better locked in our inner vault. And while God's law is intended to lead us into wholehearted living, we sometimes misuse the law in a way that leads to a split personality, a kind of "Jekyll and Hyde" spirituality that leaves us spiritually vacant, relationally disconnected, emotionally conflicted.

I saw this occur at an almost epidemic level when I lived and worked as a therapist in Orlando, Florida, the epicenter of many Christian ministries in the United States. Often I'd receive phone calls from Christians involved in various evangelical ministries whose lives were coming apart at the seams. I began to observe a pattern emerging that I could not ignore: by their late twenties and early thirties, these men and women were burning out. Their relationships were exploding. An early enthusiasm that led them into ministry had waned, leaving big questions that the basic discipleship materials they promoted could not answer. They had staked their Christian identity on the essential principles and patterns of ministry they had learned from leaders before them, but these principles couldn't touch places of deeper pain, struggle, sin, and heartache.

While these ministries provided training, mentoring, and leadership skills, those skills turned out to be inadequate to sustain young ministry workers for the long haul. Most of these men and women learned early on the demand of godly obedience; externally, they lived exemplary lives. They read their Bibles and told people about Jesus and attended church regularly. But they lacked the inner resources to counter feelings of failure, insecurity, and disappointment.

Sam was a star in one Orlando-based ministry. Extroverted, charming, and smart, at twenty-eight he had led many people to faith in Christ. When he called me on the recommendation of a friend, he was in Orlando to meet with the head of the organization. "Pastor, my marriage is dying. Shelley and I have been married for three years, and she's threatening to leave me. It would kill my entire ministry. Can you help?"

"Are you asking me to help save your ministry or save your marriage?" I asked.

"Well, I have leaders who depend on me," he said. "But my marriage is very, very important."

Sam was calling me for a quick fix to a big mess. Having lived his entire Christian life relying on tried-and-true rules, he couldn't understand why these rules had failed him now. Like many other young Christians in his situation, Sam had mistaken dutiful obedience for a life of integrity. He had become divided at his core. On the outside was a man admired by everyone. On the inside was an angry, insecure, emotionally immature boy who hid from public exposure.

One could argue that the primary problem Jesus had with the Pharisees and Jewish religious leaders of his day was that their obedience was disobedient. Their faith had become an externalized ritual, a form of religion that betrayed an inner vacancy (see Matthew 6). They'd taken the good law of Sinai and twisted it into a code that excluded, indicted, and judged others. On the outside they were squeaky clean, but on the inside they were rotting (Matthew 23:27). They thought all was well, but in reality they were dying inside. Jesus said to the Pharisees, "Go and learn what this means, 'I desire mercy, not sacrifice.' For I have come to call not the righteous but sinners" (Matthew 9:13).

The Pharisees' brand of disobedient obedience may seem like a proper response to a holy God, but it actually closes us off to the covenant grace that most deeply characterizes God's relationship with us. It sucks the life out of us, cutting us off from parts of ourselves that need to be exposed to the light of God's love. As Sam committed to the work of counseling, he emerged as a vibrant man with ample emotional resources for his family as well as his ministry. Early in his ministry, Sam's inability to have fun, to play, had choked out his ability to ride out life's successes and failures in the sure love of his heavenly Father. It took time for Sam to discover the poise of grace, an inner sense of harmony that broke down old divisions and led to a wholehearted life.

The law, by itself, was never meant to be the answer to our needs. When we seek wholeness through external conformity to the law, we miss its real point. Eugene Peterson takes a bit of liberty in his translation of Romans 8, but makes a point nonetheless: "The law always ended up being used as a Band-Aid on sin instead of a deep healing of it. And now what the law code asked for but we couldn't deliver is accomplished as we, instead of redoubling our own efforts, simply embrace what the Spirit is doing in us" (Romans 8:4, *The Message*).

In other words, while the law is good, it does not bring the real healing our hearts need because none of us are capable of keeping it perfectly. If we mistake obedience to the law for wholeness and righteousness, we get outward conformity instead of the wholehearted love that motivates true obedience. Sam began to see and experience this for himself.

An Honest Look Within

"Sin lives in a costume; that's why it is so hard to recognize," writes pastor and therapist Paul Tripp. "You'll never understand sin's sleight of hand until you recognize that the DNA of sin is deception . . . that we are all very committed and gifted self-swindlers."[1]

Part of Sam's healing required that he see the depths of his inner division. For many years he had lived out of an image of Christian obedience that demanded that any undesirable part of himself go into hiding. The hard work of therapy required a new and deeper honesty with God, with others, and with himself. Sam had a shining moment when he looked at his wife and said, "I've been an incredibly deceptive man, keeping large parts of myself away from you. I'm ashamed and sorry."

C. S. Lewis writes, "We are not merely imperfect creatures who must be improved, we are . . . rebels who must lay down our arms."[2] As we saw in the last chapter, this is a tough lesson to learn for those of us who are addicted to certainty and control. Certainly the Israelites were no exception. While Egypt revealed Israel's status as an enslaved and oppressed people, Sinai revealed an even deeper slavery to self-justification and self-salvation.

God's way of showing Israel her self-deception was to point to an outer conformity devoid of a heart rightly motivated. God's real goal was heart change: "For you have no delight in sacrifice; if I were to give a burnt offering, you would not be pleased. The sacrifice acceptable to God is a broken spirit; a broken and contrite heart, O God, you will not despise" (Psalm 51:16-17).

While God gave Israel the law to show how to order her relationships, her civil life, and her worship, all for her ultimate flourishing and good, Israel twisted that law as a means of manipulating God. And so do we.

Old Testament scholar Stephen Dempster says, "Sinai, not Egypt, is Israel's largest roadblock to Canaan."[3] What he means is this: Sometimes the best things, the most noble things, even the most "religious" things can become obstacles to real flourishing in our lives. Sometimes our journey to find God in wilderness places requires that we strip away these external forms of religion for the God who reveals himself when we are at our most needy.

I've spoken with men and women who have spent years praying consistently, attending church regularly, and living faithfully only to admit to a dry, lifeless faith. Perplexed, they wonder why God doesn't show up when they do their part. Spiritual fitness programs that emphasize our ability to master a system or strategize a seamless course through life's obstacles promise spiritual success. But wiser voices throughout the centuries have offered a distinctly different perspective.

Around the third century after Christ, men and women left the city to enter the desert. These desert mothers and fathers were not looking merely to escape the easy pleasures of urban life but to create space to let God look deeply into their hearts. Their stories continue to invite us to attend to our souls, humbly and honestly.

> A brother in Scetis committed a fault. A council was called to which Moses was invited, but he refused to go to it. Then the priest sent someone to him, saying, "Come, for everyone is waiting for you." So he got up and went. He took a sack, filled it with sand and cut a small hole at the bottom and carried it on his shoulders. The others came out to meet him and said, "What is this, father?" The Abba said to them, "My sins run out behind me, and I do not see them, and today I am coming to judge the errors of another."

When they heard that, they said no more to the brother but forgave him.[4]

Deeply embedded in the Reformed tradition is the notion that God's law isn't just a formula for spiritual success but a teacher of sin. We're not just victims of an evil outside of us, enabling us to point at others. Sinai points the finger at us. Those who see themselves as victims, at some level, must reckon with their own self-sabotage. "The enemy," writes Allender, "is in the victim, leading to broken relationships, loneliness, depression . . . and frightening rage."[5]

I was struck many years ago while reading Viktor Frankl, holocaust survivor, prolific writer, and renowned psychologist. Of all people, Frankl appears to have every reason to see others as the problem and claim his own innocence in the face of the evils perpetrated on him and his fellow Jews. And yet, with moving humility and honesty, he writes, "In the final analysis it becomes clear that the sort of person a prisoner became was the result of an inner decision, and not the result of camp influences alone."[6]

But it's not just those who see themselves as victims who need this. Successful people, professionals, politicians and pastors, people who have mastered the art of looking good, are especially vulnerable to this spiritual self-deception. Perhaps we've witnessed the moral failure of so many of them because, like us, they live with divided hearts, parading around with shiny public personas but hiding failure and brokenness. It is only as we honestly admit our weakness and failure that Sinai's navigation instructions for our journey become clear, leading us to freedom.

In a poem about the joyful and life-giving reality of keeping the law, the psalmist writes, "I run in the path of your commands, for you have set my heart free" (Psalm 119:32, 1984 NIV). Obedience to God's law sets us free—it is set like a jewel in the engagement ring of God's grace, which turns obedience from obligation to delight.

It's tempting for us to see the law as a negative thing. The friend I mentioned at the beginning of this chapter viewed the Old Testament as full of law and obligation and Jesus as full of love and non-judgmental tolerance. This is, of course, a caricature. Jesus restores the law to its proper place (Matthew 5:17-20). Love fulfills the law.

When Moses came down from Sinai, he brought back with him the most progressive and radical rule of life in the entire ancient Near East. God gave Israel a law that would govern just relations between people (Exodus 20); preserve rights for women, slaves, and strangers (Exodus 21); envision right social relations (Exodus 22); invite respect for aliens and strangers (Exodus 23:9); and engender respect and stewardship over the land (Exodus 23:10-13). Far from limiting freedom, it aimed to set God's newly liberated people free to flourish.

In the many laws governing morality, civil life, and worship, God's intent is the "re-Edening" of the world. While the first Eden was lost in humanity's failure to embrace God's vision for freedom, God set his sights on a new Eden, a promised land where God would once again dwell with his beloved people. The carefully crafted plan for a tabernacle in the last chapters of Exodus is the architectural picture of God's desire to dwell with people. The whole intent of God's law is to restore people into a loving relationship with God and with one another.

While "disobedient obedience" aims for external conformity and public holiness, God's larger design invites a kind of free obedience that opens our hearts to live into God's noble vision of life together. Justice, right relations, stewardship of the land, debt forgiveness, and love mark the obedient life of a Christian. It's a vision that demands a heartfelt commitment to love difficult people—enemies, immigrants, or ex-wives—and requires the kind of humility that makes us willing to lay down our life for the sake of another. It's the very life of the triune God, the community of love at the heart of the universe.

Sinai challenges us to rethink our mistaken forms of religiosity and to live into God's larger vision for flourishing. And as we begin to live in the freedom of God's gracious law, we may begin to experience its delightful roominess, its deep-down liberation.

Discussion

1. What do you think of my friend's critique of Christianity?

2. How does external conformity manifest in a kind of inner division? How have you experienced it?

3. What do you think it means to take an honest look at our lives? What's the point?

4. How does the law point to a life of flourishing? How does it represent our deepest yearning for life together?

Part 3

*

Wilderness:
Entering the
Furnace of
Transfor-
mation

Chapter 9

Driven into the Darkness

The pupil comes to the rebbe and asks, "Why does Torah tell us to 'place these words upon your hearts'? Why does it not say to place these holy words in our hearts?" The rebbe answers, "It is because as we are, our hearts are closed, and we cannot place the holy words in our hearts. So we place them on top of our hearts. And there they stay, until one day, the heart breaks, and the words fall in."[1] —*Desert Fathers*

I suffer your terrors; I am desperate. —*Psalm 88:15*

✳✳✳

Israel couldn't have anticipated this. After experiencing the thrill of Sinai and entering into covenant with God—a desert? Old Testament scholar Dempsey writes, "As soon as the journey from Sinai to the land of promise commences, the people move from disaster to disaster, or, in the telling place names given to the first few stops along the way, from 'Fiery Blaze' (Numbers 11:3) to 'Graveyard' (Numbers 11:34)."[2]

This is exactly how life sometimes seems for us. "Fiery Blaze" and "Graveyard" seem just right in connection with our own painful desert moments. What would the Israelites have been thinking when they entered this wilderness graveyard? We know. We know as we look at our own lives, as we consider our own pain.

I know it as I look back on my own journey. I had spent a lot of time at Sinai, where I enjoyed the comforts of being a Christian with a neatly packaged faith. While my friends in high school were reading *Sports Illustrated* and *Mad Magazine*, I started reading theology. In college I majored in philosophy, reading an even broader array of writers, from Kierkegaard to Derrida. If you read enough of this stuff, you begin to think you're really smart. As I discovered later, you begin to think that you are one of the few deep thinkers in the world. I took this attitude with me into seminary.

About fifteen years ago, during a break in my seminary training, I spent a summer at Oxford University with a New Testament scholar, a man whose recommendation would mean admission into Oxford's Ph.D. program. All the intellectual firepower I had developed now became focused on this summer of hard labor. Each week for six weeks I worked to produce a twenty-page research paper. And each week my anxiety grew. Would I make it? Was I good enough?

I didn't realize it at the time, but my anxiety was not as much about getting into Oxford as it was about winning the respect of my seminary peers and my family, and about meeting my inner need to feel worthwhile. That summer I was gaining the praises of my tutor but losing my sanity. When I returned to Orlando, I ended up in a therapist's office.

"Chuck, you're a mess," the therapist remarked, looking intently into my eyes. He went on to describe the fortress of certitude that I had been building over the years. He recognized the accomplishments but also pointedly noted the cost.

He told me that I looked and acted strangely weary for a twenty-seven-year-old on the verge of success. As he talked about the heavy burden I was carrying and the anxiety of a constant need to perform, tears of recognition began to spill from my eyes. He said, "My recommendation is that you postpone Oxford and spend another year in Orlando. You need to be in counseling. And perhaps you can even tack on a counseling degree while you're here."

He knew I was a sucker for letters next to my name. "Tack on a counseling degree" was code for "I don't want you to think this sacrifice will be worthless."

I had already purchased Oxford hats, sweatshirts, mugs, and more. But in the next hour, this man deconstructed me. He saw through the façade and dared to invite me to something more. I'd pitched my tent at Sinai, living on a diet of certainty and moralism, and he was inviting me to risk leaving it for a time of extraordinary uncertainty. Though it seemed contrary to every instinct, I packed my belongings and began the descent into the desert.

A Furnace That Transforms

Mark's description of Jesus' wilderness experience is striking: "And the Spirit immediately drove him out into the wilderness" (Mark 1:12). Drove him? Was he unwilling? Afraid? Some people enter the wilderness willingly. Others enter kicking and screaming. I suspect that most of us experience aspects of both. We know we need God in a new and deeper way, but it's hard to let go of Sinai.

The day of my meeting with the therapist was a day of both incredible grief and unimaginable hope. I'm not sure anyone else in my life knew how screwed up I was. Too immature to recognize that marriage requires honesty, I had kept my anxiety from my wife, Sara. Like most North Americans, I grew up in an environment where pain was to be avoided at all costs, and I had learned creative ways to numb myself whenever it showed up. Yet this therapist was inviting me into the painful darkness where the geography of the soul was characterized by regions of "Fiery Blaze" and "Graveyard" stillness. Part of me was scared out of my wits. But another part was alive with a new sense of adventure. This man *knew* me. For the first time, I was known, known well enough for me to trust a path of adventure even greater than Oxford.

If we're fortunate, wise souls forge the way ahead of us, calling us into further and deeper places of maturity. Roger became that wilderness guide for me in those early days. A white-haired man who rose six inches above me, Roger welcomed me with arms wide open into clinical supervision. No one can take the wilderness journey for you, but there are people who can walk alongside, helping you navigate the rough terrain along the way. For the next three years, Roger played that role for me, welcoming my questions, patiently enduring my hopeless moments, and pointing out my frequent cravings for the false security of Egypt and the false certainty of Sinai. Always he welcomed me and left me with a hug, sensing my need for this tangible reassurance.

I had my doubts. A few months prior I had been studying apocalyptic literature in the Bodleian Library at Oxford; now I was spending time with women with tyrannical husbands, men owned by their addictions, and victims of abuse entrusting me with extraordinary stories of betrayal and grief. Had I thrown away a chance to get one of the best degrees in the world for this?

One Thursday night I had a late session scheduled, forcing me to miss my favorite sitcom. It took everything in me to not cancel my 8:00 appointment. But the appointment was with a new client, and I was dutiful enough to keep it. I'd stay—but I didn't have to like it.

At five minutes past the hour, I began to feel a sense of relief. Maybe my new client had chickened out, or perhaps he'd forgotten. He showed up, however, unapologetically late. Truth be told, once the session got started, I could run on automatic. I knew how to reflect statements back, how to insert an appropriate "Hmmm," how to ask an open-ended question or two. This hour would fly by, I thought.

My client was a twenty-six-year-old man whose smug demeanor immediately irritated me. As I introduced myself, he barely made eye contact. "Here are the intake forms," he grunted. "I filled out about half. I'm not telling you all my personal information." He seemed as happy to be there as I was. I was sure he wanted to get out as much as I did, and I was very sure he'd never come again.

"I'm here because I have to be," he told me, pulling out a manila folder from a brown briefcase. In it was a letter from his wife. He handed it to me and said, "You'll get what a freak she is when you read it."

I began to read. For the next ten minutes I took in every word of an absorbing narrative that read like a tragic novel. Occasionally I glanced up, seeing before me a shell. This man had no regard for his wife—a woman who had poured herself out, who had clearly agonized over every word. He thought she was a freak. With each word I read, the man seemed more cruel. I could almost feel his cold presence. I was no longer numb, no longer thinking of Thursday night comedies or the six-pack waiting for me in the fridge. I was thinking of my own wife, Sara. I was thinking that if I were even half as cold as this man, I had damaged her beyond repair. I read the letter, and read it again. The man hadn't come to talk anyway.

For many years, I thought that obedience meant a strong-willed compliance to godly norms. I believed that God was more interested in doctrinal certainty than in a contrite spirit. That night, my heart broke. It broke not with tears or any grand display of emotion. It broke quietly within as I read that letter. It broke as I looked up to see a man devoid of emotion, going through the motions, completely unmoved by this desperate letter from his wife.

Just like me, I thought.

I no longer knew it was Thursday. I no longer thought about my favorite television shows. And while this client had no clue about what was happening, I knew very well that I was changing, that something sacred was taking place. I was dying.

This is the death that beckons us in the wilderness. It is a preparatory kind of brokenness that makes the heart ready for God's deeper work. And even while darkness closes in, a corresponding hopefulness begins to dawn.

Step by step, a new life began to emerge—this time not in approval from a prestigious institution or satisfaction in meeting other's expectations, but in wilderness brokenness. I began to understand the upside-down logic of Jesus' words "Very truly, I tell you, unless a grain of wheat falls into the earth and dies, it remains just a single grain; but if it dies, it bears much fruit" (John 12:24).

A Furnace That Scorches

For some, the wilderness comes as an opportunity for transformation, a brokenness that leads to life. For others, however, the wilderness offers nothing but terror, confusion, and painful suffering. Instead of appearing as a beacon of light, it comes as a storm, a torrent, a dagger, a fiery blaze that does not seem to hold any hope for transformation.

Mark, a lawyer, was married to Janna, his college sweetheart, and was the proud father of three children. Both in their late thirties, life had treated Mark and Janna well. Three weeks earlier, if you'd asked them if they'd ever experienced struggle in their fifteen years of marriage, they might have pointed to Mark's premature balding. Aside from that, life was good. Their oldest son was an extraordinary musician at the age of thirteen. Their daughter led her basketball team in scoring and was bound for athletic stardom. The youngest boy was a thriving fourth grader immersed in video games, baseball, and guitar lessons. Mark and Janna led a small group at their church, where both were known as extraordinary people—gracious, hospitable, and humble. Their marriage was an inspiration to younger and older couples alike.

Then Janna received the diagnosis. Breast cancer. Both her mother and her grandmother had succumbed to the same disease before they were fifty. Janna had come to faith in Christ in college, the first of her agnostic family to do so. Somehow, she thought, her faith would prevent the seemingly inevitable. When Mark and Janna entered my office, I could feel the weight of their pain. They looked like a couple already resigned to a certain conclusion.

I knew of Mark and Janna through their extraordinary reputation. Their pastor once told me, "They're as solid as you get." But today they were undone. They held hands as Janna recounted the events of the past couple of weeks with a good degree of composure. But then came the big questions. Why? Why would God do this? Why would God not spare Janna, a Christian and a mother? Why them? These questions were raised in a tone of disbelief. Janna wasn't saying, "I'm a great Christian; I should be spared." Rather, she was staring at death stalking her in the middle of an extraordinary life, and she could not fathom it.

In this wilderness valley of the shadow of death, Janna was perplexed, confused, unsure if she even knew this God who had once seemed so gracious. Mark was angry and felt betrayed by God. Neither would show up for church that Sunday, or for several months afterward. What would be the point?

The wilderness is a place of chaos and darkness. And for all of the platitudes Christians and non-Christians alike can offer, very little can tame the anger of a man whose wife will die of cancer. Nor should it. In these moments, God does seem unconcerned, arbitrary, even cruel. And even if our theological questions could be answered, the pain doesn't go away. As much as we believe that God can redeem our journey through the wilderness, we should never underestimate its destructive force. Driven into his own wilderness, Job cries, "Let the day perish in which I was born, and the night that said, 'A man-child is conceived.' Let that day be darkness! May God above not seek it, or light shine on it. Let gloom and deep darkness claim it. Let clouds settle upon it; let the blackness of the day terrify it" (Job 3:3-5).

It's a typically North American phenomenon to glamorize suffering. As I write, doctors and commentators are marveling at the miraculous recovery of Congresswoman Gabrielle Giffords, who was shot in the head by an assassin. The media highlights her heroism. But in the same tragedy, a nine-year-old girl lost her life. For her there was no happy ending. A reporter attempts to spin her death as a victory for another patient who received a kidney from the victim. But the little girl's parents are left only with grief.

The psalmist groans, "I suffer your terrors; I am desperate" (88:15).

Wilderness darkness. It's when the bottom falls out. It's when everything you knew to be true is called into question. It's when the "answers" provide no comfort. Security is stripped. Your sense of justice is offended.

When the Israelites had come up out of Egypt, they cried, "Was it because there were no graves in Egypt that you have taken us away to die in the wilderness? What have you done to us, bringing us out of Egypt?" (Exodus 14:11).

Sometimes the wilderness invites grief, nothing but grief. Sinai's certainties provide no balm. God's promise of presence provides no refuge. Even Jesus, facing the darkness, could not help but cry out, "My God, my God, why have you forsaken me?" (Matthew 27:46). He was quoting Psalm 22, and some commentators argue that in this context, there is hope, even resolution. The gospel writers, however, don't resolve the grief for us.

Perhaps our uniquely North American propensity to find some bright side to pain needs to be modified by the voices of Job, of the Psalms, of all who lament, including Jesus. For Mark and Janna, and for many others, the wilderness is not a spiritual adventure or a lesson in courage. It is hell on earth, a hell that feels never-ending. And in moments like these we find the words of a psalmist whose pain did not resolve, words that resonate with us in their haunting truthfulness: "Darkness is my closest friend" (Psalm 88:18, NIV).

Discussion

1. In this chapter, wilderness is experienced in two different ways: one that expresses hope and another that knows only darkness. In which ways have you encountered either or both of those wilderness experiences?

2. If you have not experienced a wilderness experience, how does this chapter make you feel about it?

3. What is your ordinary response to pain or suffering in another person's life? Is your tendency to cast a positive spin on it? How might listening to another person talk about his or her pain make you uncomfortable or unsure of how to respond?

4. How does it make you feel to read a psalm or a chapter of a Christian book that ends without a sense of resolution?

Chapter 10

Kleenex Theology

In our private lives, we need safe relationships in which we can explore our inner turmoil, small-scale communities where we can get help from others in naming our illusions and absorbing and transforming our suffering. —Parker Palmer

Following Christ is a hard road, but little by little you will see the light in the darkness and drink the water that springs from a dry land. —John Goldingay

***

I don't do suffering well. In fact, I despise it. My first response to my daughters' tears is "How do I fix this?" I've been habituated to respond to suffering with action or answers. And I'm not the only one. It's a North American phenomenon. We're uncomfortable with awkward silence and even more uncomfortable with unresolved pain.

We seem to be so civil in our response to suffering. A slight tear brings out the Kleenex, and the mess is wiped clean. We expect that any crisis will be met with a clear-headed solution; a national trauma is turned into a celebration of courage.

Even Christians whose roots go deep into the soil of suffering seem to know little about walking in and through it.

Some churches teach that faith is a kind of antibody to suffering, guarding true believers from pain. Others acknowledge the inevitability of suffering, even among the faithful, but provide little language for expressing it. As modern North American Christians, we've lost that wilderness edge, and in the process we've lost solidarity with the many saints around the world who are suffering today and the millions who have suffered before us.

Denying the reality of suffering, we seek to evade the possibility that we might have to dive into an uncivilized grief or weep tears that refuse to be quenched. We dare not imagine any scenario in which suffering could not be alleviated, preferring to believe that in our world there is a fix for everything. Many years ago, I was counseling a woman who began crying. Her cries became deeper and deeper, emerging from a place that few are willing to access. In her grief she grew louder and more animated, saying words most people think should not be spoken in a church building. Later a fellow church staff member came by and asked what was going on. When I told him, he said, "Wow! I almost called the police."

He was alarmed by this woman's expression of her suffering. As I was sitting with her, I was alarmed too. I was worried about what to say and what to do. I was worried about what my colleagues might think. I wondered if God was all right with this much honesty.

Over the years, however, I've become convinced that this is the honest language of the Exodus road. Lament, the ancient art of crying out before God, provides us with a means of honest and raw expression in times when our grief is too much to bear. It does not offer a quick fix or a tidy theological answer.

Rather, it invites us to bring ourselves fully to a God who can handle our pain, perhaps more than we've ever imagined.

Complaining or Lamenting?

If we turn back to the Exodus story, however, all this talk of permission to lament seems false.

> Then all the congregation raised a loud cry, and the people wept that night. And all the Israelites complained against Moses and Aaron; the whole congregation said to them, "Would that we had died in the land of Egypt! Or would that we had died in this wilderness! Why is the LORD bringing us into this land to fall by the sword? Our wives and our little ones will become booty; would it not be better for us to go back to Egypt?" So they said to one another, "Let us choose a captain, and go back to Egypt" (Numbers 14:1-4).

What was God's response to their cry? "How long will these people treat me with contempt? How long will they refuse to believe in me . . . ? I will strike them down with a plague and destroy them" (Numbers 14:11-12, NIV). What's going on here? God invites our honest cries, and Jesus himself demonstrates lament by shouting, "My God, my God, why have you forsaken me?" (Matthew 27:46). But God angrily disciplines Israel as if God were incapable of absorbing their complaints. How can we understand this?

We can begin by looking again at how Christians in our culture have learned to deal with pain and suffering. We typically zero in on the apostle Paul, who encouraged the Philippians to "do everything without grumbling or arguing" (Philippians 2:14, NIV). Just two chapters later he urges the Philippians to "rejoice in the Lord always" (4:4). From this advice we conclude that grumbling or complaining is bad and rejoicing is good. Many of my clients over the years have taken these commands to heart, believing that God would never accept their honest struggle with him.

But we often miss the important distinction between complaint and lament. When the Israelites complained to God, their minds were made up. They were ready to return to Egypt, to choose someone other than God to lead them. Instead of engaging God honestly in the midst of their suffering, they chose to turn their backs and hightail it back to the land where they could resume their relatively comfortable enslavement. It's this refusal to engage honestly in relationship that angers God. We know this because the Bible is full of raw anger and honest questioning toward God. Lament is almost a spiritual art form. But complaining, faithlessly turning one's back to God, leads to the kind of tragic discipline Israel would receive from God on their Exodus journey.

One who laments often looks like a grumbler or complainer, writes Dan Allender, but biblical lament is nothing of the sort. Instead, lament contains in itself the possibility of extraordinary hope, restored desire, and a changed heart. At its core, he says, lament is a search for God. It is not a search for answers or an invitation to fix an ailment. Rather, lament enters the agony with the recognition that it might not go away for days, months, even years. And yet, it carries the hope that God will eventually show up. He writes, "Lament is a search—a declaration of desire that will neither rest with a pious refusal to ache, nor an arrogant self-reliance that is a hardened refusal to search."[1]

The difference between complaint and lament depends on our entire orientation toward God—complaining, we give up on God; in our lament we trust God with our deepest suffering and fears.

Grief Not Disguised

"If I'd wanted my pain theologized away, I would have gone to Job's friends." So said a client early in my clinical counseling internship. Her comment struck me dumb. She needed Jesus, God-in-the-flesh, the Suffering Servant who left the comforts of heaven to engage suffering face to face. Instead she got a theologian, a triage medic of the soul who applied Bible verses, made generalizations that missed her specific pain, and offered platitudes. I had failed her, but she'd had the courage to speak up.

In God's ironic grace, my failure was the gateway to her renewed journey of hope. She had spoken honestly not only to her counselor but to a minister, a spiritual leader like those who had been responsible for beating hope out of her for so many years. The child of a pastor, this woman had known only spiritual platitudes and polite interactions. She had known only a gospel of principles for better living. Never challenged to think on her own, never encouraged to speak her doubts, she had lived a lonely, isolated life. Referred by her pastor, her presenting problem was depression. Categorized, isolated, marginalized, and referred to a professional for help, she had begun to believe the message her church was feeding her: "You're too messy. When you get better, we'll invite you back. But get help first."

One of the reasons we may fail to lament is that there are so few safe people around to receive it. God certainly hears our cries, but God also made us in and for relationship. The church is the place where our personal laments can join the choir of hurt that sings its off-tune chorus before God. We need friends in tough times, men and women willing to sit in the pain with us. As Parker Palmer writes,

> In our private lives, we need safe relationships in which we can explore our inner turmoil, small-scale communities where we can get help from others in naming our illusions and absorbing and transforming our suffering. In such relationships, we must learn to resist the gravitational force of conventional culture, to resist especially the constant temptation to "fix" or "save" the other person. Instead, we must learn to listen deeply and ask honest, open questions, cultivating the trust that meaningful responses to suffering can come only from within the one who suffers.[2]

In Christian subcultures where suffering may be interpreted as a lack of faith we learn to disguise our pain, conveying a false self that betrays who we really are and what we're really feeling. As it turns out, humans have been doing this for millennia. Faced with the tortuous theological ramblings of his fix-it friends, Job rejects their Kleenex theology: "My brothers are as undependable as intermittent streams. . . . Now you too have proved to be of no help; you see something dreadful and are afraid. . . . Teach me, and I will be quiet; show me where I have been wrong. How painful are honest words! But what do your arguments prove? Do you mean to correct what I say, and treat my desperate words as wind?" (Job 6:15, 21, 24-26, NIV).

Job needed friends to engage the pain, not interpret the pain. He needed friends who would join the chorus of lament, not offer a recipe for a more faithful life. In the end, Job is commended for his honesty while his theologically correct buddies are scolded for their insensitivity. God does not want us to disguise ourselves, hiding the pain we feel so deeply.

God in the Details

The history of Israel is replete with wilderness intrusions. Like us, Israel experienced highs and lows, riding the roller coaster of blessing and brokenness. Of the many dark times in her history, the destruction of Jerusalem in 586 B.C. tops the list. In fact, an entire book of the Bible—the book of Lamentations—is devoted to expressing Israel's grief.

The details are messy. Israel "weeps bitterly in the night" (Lamentations 1:2). Her "young girls grieve" (1:4), her enemies mock her nakedness (1:8), her neighbors have betrayed her (1:17). God seems not like a safe place but like an enemy (2:5). There are gruesome images of utter desperation: hungry children (2:19), mothers eating their children (2:20), the slaughter of young and old (2:21). Human rights have become "perverted" (3:35): women are raped (5:11) and men are abused (5:13). Israel feels utterly abandoned. The book ends with a sentiment to which many who have experienced the darkness can relate: "Restore us to yourself, O LORD, that we may be restored . . . unless you have utterly rejected us" (5:20-22).

But a deeper level of structural detail reveals how God, like a good counselor, wants to hear each and every whisper and cry of Israel's suffering. Eugene Peterson describes the form of Lamentations as a series of five acrostics (much like Psalm 119). Acrostics are literary patterns that travel through the alphabet slowly, in meticulous detail, from beginning to end. Beginning at the Hebrew *aleph* and ending at its last letter *tau*, lament proceeds through each letter with careful and extraordinarily honest expression. Five times in five distinct poems the writer revisits his pain, most often in communal expression, with a brief interlude for private weeping. In other words, God's invitation is clear. Every detail of pain is important. Every ounce of grief must be squeezed out. Pain must be expressed honestly, both privately and communally.[3]

How radical is this? Imagine having God's permission to get it all out: the anger, the betrayal, the injustice. Imagine God's Spirit, often called Counselor, offering space to grieve your pain from A to Z. Imagine God's interest in hearing it all, not just the general story but every little detail. Now consider how far from this practice we are today. Psychologist David Benner argues that in large part, the rise of therapy has resulted from the church's abdication of soul care in order to focus on intellectual debates.[4] As a result, many churches are not safe spaces where we can bring every detail of our pain before God, and many pastors are inadequately prepared to offer the care that pain requires.

Interestingly, neurosis is often defined as the denial of reality. Perhaps providing a context for lament might be a way to alleviate the neurosis of a culture that feeds on false reality and virtual reality. Churches that deny a place for lament, referring the wounded to "clinical care," are burying their heads in the sand of false reality. That is not to diminish or question the important role of clinical counseling as a ministry among and for Christians. But too often the referral reflects an inability or refusal to walk through the timely and messy acrostic of suffering from *aleph* to *tau*. Perhaps also it reflects a fear that corporate lament in worship does not produce the kind of "positive" environment our culture is so apt to prefer.

The grave danger is that in denying the opportunity for lament on our wilderness roads, we only perpetuate dishonesty, cheap solutions, and a view of God that does not fit the complex realities of our messy lives.

Keeping Our Eyes on the Promised Land

God is not in the business of quenching hope. God's way, however, often traverses the longer, harder road through rough wilderness terrain. God invites us to walk on, not to turn back to Egypt where slavery's false securities await.

In his book *Walk On*, Old Testament scholar John Goldingay talks about his own grief and agony walking alongside his wife, Ann, who battles multiple sclerosis. One might think that as a theologian steeped in the Bible, John has all of the answers. But answers elude him. It's not as if there are no answers, he argues. It's just that we don't know, and that not-knowing can be agonizing. Goldingay wrestles with all of the issues any husband might wrestle with as he watches his wife suffer. He writes, "Following Christ is a hard road, but little by little you will see the light in the darkness and drink the water that springs from a dry land."[5]

Sometimes we make the mistake of confusing prog-ress with hope. Progress offers me the iPhone and digestive enzymes for my gluten allergy. Progress allows me to trust my GPS when I'm lost. Progress is splitting the atom, decoding the human genome, and finding sustainable ways of living. It is often a very good thing. But progress can also steal away our capacity for trust and erode our capacity for hope.

Could it be that in Egypt Israel had learned the ways of the empire, with its many technologies and securities, only to find itself completely lost when those things failed? Could it be that the things we call *progressive* might actually lead us in the opposite direction of dependence, trust, and hope?

Mark and Janna, the couple I wrote about in the previous chapter, were heartened by Janna's prognosis through surgery and radiation, but they were not spared the everyday wilder-ness of uncertainty. They did not get answers to their ques-tions, but they did experience the simple grace of being able to place one foot in front of the other, walking on toward the ultimate hope of a land where there will be no more tears (Revelation 21:4).

Not long after Janna's final radiation treatment, she showed up in church. She sat in the back with Mark by her side. Her kids were glad to be back, reconnecting with friends and devouring the cookies and juice in the fellowship room. That Sunday their pastor was talking about heaven. Mark and Janna were a bit worried that they'd be fed a diet of easy answers, but that wasn't the case. Instead their pastor quoted a verse they'd never heard before. It was the cry of the saints who'd been martyred and were with Jesus even now: "Sovereign Lord, holy and true, how long will it be before you judge and avenge our blood on the inhabitants of the earth?" (Revelation 6:10).

Mark and Janna looked at one another. They had learned the language of lament well. "How long?" had been on their lips over and over again throughout the past weeks. Tears came to their eyes.

Even the saints in heaven lament.

In my office the following Tuesday, it struck me that they had made their way from A to Z. No doubt, there'd be more grief along the way. But somehow they had journeyed through the alphabet of pain, finding that Sunday morning their *tau*, that final letter that brought some measure of peace and hope and even trust. In the previous weeks, they had expressed lament before God that many churchgoers might consider heresy. Their words were harsh and painfully honest. God had listened, and they knew it. And while that didn't make the pain or the cancer go away, it brought them some measure of joy.

The world we live in now is a wilderness where faith is tested and hope keeps us moving toward the promised land, step by often painful step. Even those ahead of us may lament on our behalf. But they are also cheering for us to "run with perseverance the race that is set before us . . ." (Hebrews 12:1). There is a promised land where every tear will be wiped away and pain and death will be no more (Revelation 21:4-5). That's not a palliative—it's a promise, a promise that keeps us going along the wilderness road.

Discussion

1. This chapter suggests that the typical American pattern is to bypass suffering and grief in favor of optimism and positive thinking. How have you experienced this?

2. What is the difference between lament and complaint? Think of some examples of each.

3. Why is it important to bring every detail of our grief to God? How does the Bible validate doing so?

4. What are the safe places for you to express this kind of lament? Is your church safe? Why or why not?

Chapter 11

The Grasshopper Effect

We seemed like grasshoppers in our own eyes, and we looked
the same to them.

—*Numbers 13:33, NIV*

Self-doubt is a cruel and crippling emotion. It robs its victims of security, dignity, composure, and resourcefulness. To remain in cowering self-doubt is to distrust God.

—*Raymond Brown*

Israel rejects God not because they want to be more,
but rather because they are willing to settle for less.

—*David Stubbs*

✳✳✳

Pride goes before a fall.

So says the wise writer of Proverbs. And so this has proven to be the case over and again. Countless stories of corrupt leaders show a brazen narcissism birthed by a bloated self-image. The former governor of New York is caught in the same behavior he aggressively prosecuted as attorney general. Congressmen from Idaho and Florida are caught in gay sex scandals after aggressive political attacks against homosexual rights advocates. The "family man" image of golfer Tiger Woods is obliterated amidst sordid revelations of infidelity.

Each example is a window on our human tendency toward self-bloating, a narcissistic and egocentric psychological phenomenon that cuts us off from ourselves, from others, from reality, and from God. Biblical scholar Raymond Brown echoes the writer of Proverbs: "To operate in brash self-confidence is to court disaster."[1] And we've all seen the destruction that follows pride.

But are our wilderness difficulties this easily explainable? Is self-bloating narcissism our biggest problem?

Grasshoppers in Our Own Eyes

The book of Numbers highlights the post-Sinai wilderness days of the Israelites. The problem is that after pages of census data and law-and-worship instructions, well-intentioned readers tend to start yawning, skimming, and even skipping, thus missing its climactic story.

In Numbers 13, the Israelites find themselves on the very brink of the life they had long yearned for. After leaving their homes and journeying for months through unforgiving desert terrain, they arrive at the border of the promised land. When spies are sent to scout the land, they find exactly what Moses had promised. Their description reminds me of what our family sees when we drive through the Napa Valley, that great California wine country covered in a sea of lush grapevines producing some of the best wine on earth. The scouts discover their Napa, Wadi Eshcol, the "valley of the grapes," a fruitful oasis that must have been a sight for sore eyes and hungry stomachs. There they gather a single cluster of grapes described as too heavy for one man to carry. As theologian David Stubbs writes, "The image of the scouts bringing back a cluster of grapes so large that it is hung on a pole supported by two men is a wonderful symbol of the fruitfulness of the promised land."[2]

Before the Israelites lay a sea of grapes, figs, and pomegranates, truly "a land flowing with milk and honey" (Numbers 14:8). According to Moses and by good (divine!) authority, it was all theirs for generations of enjoyment. The same God who had heard their cries, rescued them, and loved them despite their continual whining, had now delivered them to the promised land.

Any careful reader of the previous chapters of Numbers would see the possibilities. The yawn-inducing census-taking now makes sense—these people have the numbers to enter the land and conquer! The narrative swells to the climactic moment when the spies return bearing the fruit of the land and joyous news: "We came to the land to which you sent us; it flows with milk and honey, and this is its fruit" (Numbers 13:27).

This is a moment ripe with narcissistic possibilities for any pride-addicted idolater. But pride is not Israel's problem, at least not this time. The next verses expose an insidious wilderness epidemic that would infect the entire nation in short time.

But the men who had gone up with him said, "We can't attack those people; they are stronger than we are." And they spread among the Israelites a bad report about the land they had explored. They said, "The land we explored devours those living in it. All the people we saw there are of great size. We saw the Nephilim there (the descendants of Anak come from the Nephilim). We seemed like grasshoppers in our own eyes, and we looked the same to them" (Numbers 13:31-33, NIV).

We seemed like grasshoppers.

The Israelites, rescued and redeemed, called a "treasured possession," loved and chosen intentionally by Yahweh, stumbled not over a bloated sense of pride but over their despairing sense of inadequacy. Their wilderness fear arose neither from a sense of narcissistic entitlement nor from proud accomplishment but from slavery-induced self-deprecation.

Settling for Less

What caused Israel to balk on the very edge of ultimate satisfaction and restoration? Maybe we can ask ourselves the same question. What makes you return continually to the same old patterns and behaviors? What prompts you to settle for less in your closest relationships instead of fighting for more? What causes you to return to an addiction that you know hurts you and the ones you love?

Stubbs writes, "Israel rejects God not because they want to be more, but rather because they are willing to settle for less."[3] What incites this devastating choice, I believe, is not just the appalling sight of the land's large inhabitants, but also the vision of its lush fruit. It was all too much to bear. In one instant, they saw their greatest hopes and greatest fears before them. Instead of taking the risk of claiming their dreams, they chose instead to succumb to their old nemesis—self-condemnation.

The narrative of self-condemnation says, "Life is not going to get any better. You're nothing. Just give up." It feeds on shame, which is quite different than guilt. Guilt feeds on what we do wrong. Shame shouts that we *are* wrong, that we are bad, that we are nothing. It forgets God's message to Israel and to us that we are God's treasured possession.

I've seen men and women who have walked to the edge of the promised land only to see both the glory of a better life and the inevitability of utter failure.

I've seen an abused woman work for years in therapy and begin to believe that God actually loves her only to throw it all away for an affair with a married man. She told me that the closer she got to believing that God actually loved her, the harder it got to endure the shame. Her affair confirmed her lifelong narrative—that she was a slut who deserved nothing better than a man who'd use her.

I've seen a man who sabotaged every good thing in his life. Presented with an opportunity of a well-paying job to support his family, he'd sleep in, miss deadlines, and face the inevitable disappointment of his boss. Offered an opportunity to step up as a dad, he'd miss another childhood event only to experience the wrath of his disappointed wife. As much as he wanted more, he couldn't bear it.

Is his problem pride? Does she have a bloated self-image? I don't think so. Both of these people live out a narrative they learned in "slavery." Both of their childhoods were marked by disappointment, a lack of consistent love, and some form of emotional or sexual abuse. In both cases, the real tragedy is that they got so close to the promised land, even tasting the fruit, only to succumb to slavery's stranglehold.

Raymond Brown speaks to the very real threat of both a bloated self-image and an emaciated self-image:

Self-doubt is a cruel and crippling emotion. It robs its victims of security, dignity, composure, and resourcefulness. If we are to be used by [God], we must certainly begin with a realistic assessment of our limitations. To operate in brash self-confidence is to court disaster; to remain in cowering self-doubt is to distrust God.[4]

What causes Israel to stumble in the most important hour of their existence is not pride, but shame-induced sloth, another deadly sin that stifles the will to embrace the extraordinary satisfaction God offers. Stubbs writes, "As a result of their unfaithful sloth/despair, Israel turns back from entering the promised land and chooses the path of Egyptian slavery and misery over the path of courage, effort, and hope leading toward the promised land."[5]

We all know this reality, for Israel's story is our story. We know what it means to settle, to avoid stepping into God's better design for our lives. It happens in big ways, but it also happens in small and simple moments: when I've settled for a night in front of the television rather than engaging my wife in conversation, when I've believed that God has no better design for me than to endure the pain of life.

Believing we are but grasshoppers, we tend to settle for what seems possible.

Pasts That Haunt Us

In his biography of the great priest and psychologist Henri Nouwen, Michael Ford recounts Nouwen's moments of profound self-deprecation and despair. Though he tirelessly communicated a gospel of love and acceptance in God's embrace,

Nouwen himself often felt unloved. Though he worked frenetically, he felt empty when he was not busy.

> While complaining about too many demands, I felt uneasy when none were made. While speaking about the burden of letter writing, an empty mailbox made me sad. While fretting about tiring lecture tours, I felt disappointed when there were no invitations. While speaking nostalgically about an empty desk, I feared the day on which that would come true. In short: while desiring to be alone, I was frightened of being left alone.[6]

Ford shows that Nouwen's own childhood wounds ran so deep that the love of friends, family, and God could not mitigate the deep pain. Nouwen could speak unashamedly about God's passionate love for broken and wounded people, but he struggled to embrace that love for himself. On the edge of the promised land, Nouwen often retreated to old vices learned in slavery—demanding, manipulating, self-pitying his way into acceptance. Praised by so many as a spiritual giant, Nouwen felt more like a grasshopper.

I've met many outwardly successful men and women who exude confidence and even a bit of narcissism but who, deep inside, hide a grasshopper view of themselves. Jim was a successful entrepreneur who impressed everyone who knew him with his charm and confidence. Yet in my counseling office, this confident man revealed his extraordinary fears. Bullied as a young man, Jim vowed to protect himself from the harm he might experience in life. Success, he reasoned, would prevent others from challenging him. It became his best defense. He intimidated, manipulated, and guarded himself against all threats. That is, until his wife threatened to end their marriage.

The man I got to know in the weeks that followed shifted from being impenetrable to becoming vulnerable. He confessed that his wife was his "trophy," a cheerleader who began as a conquest but became the love of his life. But he also recognized that his life was driven by a fear of losing her because he felt that he didn't deserve her. He felt like a grasshopper married to a beautiful queen.

Jim's story is a common one. Though dressed like a soldier ready to conquer the promised land by force, he lived fearfully, tucking tail and running in the face of real threat. Scariest of all was a sense of being needy, dependent, fallible. Like so many of us, and like the Israelites of old, Jim lived under the power of an old story in his life—a bullied child vowing never to be vulnerable again. Our stories may be different, but so many of them follow a similar plotline. We compensate, one way or another, for the difficulties we experience early on in life. And we find ourselves living under the power of slavery rather than entering into the life God offers.

Again we find ourselves in the grip of this ancient story. In the spies' fear we find our own fear. In their retreat we see the many ways in which we retreat. In their bloated sense of the enemy's size and their diminished sense of themselves, we recognize our own inner struggles. So close to growing and maturing through difficulty, we stumble. So near resolution in a conflict, we sabotage. So eager to transcend the power of our old demons, we succumb once again.

Our greatest vulnerability isn't the bullies we face, the failures we experience, or the giants before whom we cower. Our greatest vulnerability may actually be how ready we are to settle. As writer Timothy Jones put it: "The great danger facing all of us is that someday we may wake up and find that always we have been busy with the husks and trappings of life and have really missed life itself."[7]

Wilderness Self-Compassion

The prophet Jeremiah seems to know this very human tendency to settle: "My people have committed two sins: They have forsaken me, the spring of living water, and have dug their own cisterns, broken cisterns that cannot hold water" (Jeremiah 2:13, NIV).

It's tough to realize that we've chosen broken cisterns. But it may be even more difficult to realize that we've forfeited the spring of living water. I see this every day as I spend time with people who struggle. It's one thing to confess a continual battle with an idol or addiction. Yet what brings men and women to tears is the recognition that they have forfeited a better life. How do we cope with our continual struggles and personal failures?

One thing we learn from the wilderness is that failure is inevitable. We see in Israel's story and our own that slavery's power is strong. Our pasts hold great power over us.

The Christian story tells this story of failure and difficulty too. From St. Augustine to Martin Luther to John Calvin, we hear that we are simultaneously loved by God and continually struggling with sin. John Calvin, perhaps surprisingly, promoted an extraordinary self-compassion for ordinary people who find themselves so close to the promised land yet so bent on sabotaging their own progress. Though we find ourselves "wavering and limping and even creeping along the ground," he urges us to "proceed according to the measure of [our] puny capacity and set out upon the journey we have begun."[8] For those locked in pride, these words may seem demeaning, but to those ridden with shame, they are soothing, even liberating.

George MacDonald, the great nineteenth-century pastor who profoundly influenced C. S. Lewis, conveyed his own sense of failure and renewed hope in God's love:

When I no more can stir my soul to move,
And life is but the ashes of a fire;
When I can but remember that my heart
Once used to live and love, long and aspire,
Oh, be thou then the first, the one thou art;
Be thou the calling, before all answering love,
And in me wake hope, fear, boundless desire.[9]

Faced with the daunting prospect of moving forward, of embracing a life of greater flourishing, we find ourselves losing hope. The sex addict returns to his favorite pornographic sites. The workaholic returns to his busy schedule, knowing that his schedule kills any chance of intimacy with his wife or connection with his children. The angry wife defaults to her husband's defensiveness, squelching his spirit. The abused woman returns to a relationship where she knows she'll be used rather than loved. The religious addict defaults to her legalistic ways, judging others rather than embracing the love God has for her even in her failures. Over and over again, we choose to return to Egypt instead of daring to enter the promised land. We settle for less than the life for which God made us.

Frederick Buechner is a pastor, a writer, a professor, and a wise sage. His three-part memoir is a testimony to his mistakes as a father and husband, his enduring battle with the consequences of his father's suicide, and his attempt to narrate his life through his own novels. Speaking of his own battle with the past, he writes,

> We cannot undo our old mistakes or their consequences any more than we can erase old wounds that we have both suffered and inflicted, but through the power that memory gives us of thinking, feeling, imagining our way back through time we can at long last finally finish with the past in the sense of removing its power to hurt us and other people and to stunt our growth as human beings.[10]

Buechner urges us to use our memories. The Exodus story does the same. It invites us to look back at where we've been and remember God's relentless love for us despite our many failures. It invites us to see our story as one marked by both glory and failure, and to accept the inevitability of continued struggle. It invites us to recognize our propensity to fall into the same old struggles, to admit our continued propensity to self-sabotage, and to embrace the compassion that Jesus has for us. And though our fear may lead us even more deeply into the wilderness for a time of greater struggle and refinement, our great hope is that God's enduring commitment is to make us ready—ready for the life for which we've been created, ready to become what God has intended for us to become, ready to flourish in the land flowing with milk and honey.

Despite our fear, despite our self-sabotage, God will get us there. That's God's promise to us, even in the desert, even when we've blown it, even when we feel as if there is no hope. In the words of Isaiah: "I will make rivers flow on barren heights, and springs within the valleys. I will turn the desert into pools of water, and the parched ground into springs" (41:18, NIV). What the rest of the biblical story tells us is that God never, ever gives up on us, though we continually give up on ourselves. God doesn't seem to think we're grasshoppers at all.

In fact, in Jesus God became small so that we might become great. And that's a story worth embracing.

Discussion

1. As you consider your own journey, how do you relate to the spies who balked when they saw the giants in the land? Who are your giants? How are you the "grasshopper"?

2. How is it possible for us to get so close to embracing a better life and then balk when we have that opportunity? Think of a time when you have balked in the face of God's offer of fruitfulness and flourishing.

3. George MacDonald prayed that God would awaken in him "fear, hope, and boundless desire." How can this become your prayer? What is it about your desires that you're afraid of?

Chapter 12

Cruciform Transformation

*I*sn't it the moment of most profound doubt that gives birth
to new certainties? Perhaps hopelessness is the very soil that
nourishes human hope; perhaps one could never find sense in
life without first experiencing its absurdity.   —Vaclav Havel

*Our spiritual journey must lead through the desert or else our
healing will be the product of our own will and wisdom. It is in
the silence of the desert that we hear our dependence on noise.
It is in the poverty of the desert that we see clearly our attachments to the trinkets and baubles we cling to for security and
pleasure. The desert shatters the soul's arrogance and leaves
body and soul crying out in thirst and hunger. In the desert we
trust God or die.*   —Dan Allender

"Why a wilderness?" asked my client, barely able to contain
the kind of convulsive tears that come when a person's pain
reaches deep into caverns normally inaccessible. She wasn't
looking for an answer, but for partnership in her pain.

Nevertheless, my client's question is important: Why a
wilderness?

Though the answer to that question is veiled in deep mystery, the Exodus story peels back the veil just a bit, opening us to God's heart for restoration, even if comes through difficulty, darkness, and death. Just as the Exodus is the decisive event of the Old Testament, the "exodus" of Jesus' cross and resurrection is the corresponding and fulfilling event of the New. In both, the wilderness of suffering is central. We're told that Jesus experienced the hunger and thirst of the wilderness (John 19:28), the mockery of his community (John 19:3), the injustice of abandonment (Matthew 27:46), and the relief of surrender (John 19:30). "God's solution," says theologian N. T. Wright, "is not to destroy and start from scratch, but to redeem through the new exodus, which has been accomplished in the death and resurrection of Jesus and the gift of the Spirit."[1]

Where God Shows Up

Every day, influential and well-known faith healers proclaim their message to needy crowds: "If you have faith, Jesus will heal you!" People who are struggling with overwhelming physical and emotional ailments are drawn to this, in large part, because it feels like hope in a virtually hopeless situation. In the last months before succumbing to Lou Gehrig's disease, a former student of mine was willing to try anything, contrary to his tradition. He came into my office the day before he attended a mega-church healing service, saying, "I'm willing to do anything that helps."

He died not long after, and as far as I know, he didn't regret anything he tried. People who are dying are right to put up a fight; death is an enemy, after all. But too often the conclusion some people draw when faith healing fails is that suffering comes from a lack of faith. To make matters worse, we're left to wonder if God is *blaming* us rather than *meeting* us in the pain.

Rather than seeing suffering only as a detour, a misstep, a wrong turn, we need to learn to see it as the place God meets us and the way God transforms us. Says pastor Tim Keller:

> But over and over again, God meets us in the wilderness. He meets us in the desert. When we think our life is on a detour, it's really spiritual main street. When we think everything is going wrong, it's going wrong because it forces us to think in ways we wouldn't have thought otherwise. It forces us to seek in ways we wouldn't have sought otherwise. When things aren't going according to your plan, when you think you're on a back road, it's main street spiritually.[2]

Those most closely attuned to their pain demonstrate a unique vulnerability, a vulnerability that opens them to grace. The poor in spirit inherit the kingdom; the mourners are comforted; the humbled are empowered; the thirsty are satisfied (Matthew 5:3-6). In the most extraordinary moments of brokenness, hope breaks through.

Vaclav Havel, the great Czech playwright, poet, and politician, witnessed this paradoxical reality on a national level. In fact, he helped usher it in, playing the role of Moses to the Czech people burdened under the oppressive weight of communism. Havel witnessed firsthand corruption and oppression in his beloved country. As a dissident and revolutionary, he was imprisoned for his actions, experiencing the hopelessness and pain of his own wilderness. Yet he struggled on, refusing to give up the vision of freedom. Eventually he became president of a new Czech Republic in a kind of death and resurrection for him and for the nation he loved. This experience wins him the credibility to write, "Isn't it the moment of most profound doubt that gives birth to new certainties? Perhaps hopelessness is the very soil that nourishes human hope; perhaps one could never find sense in life without first experiencing its absurdity."[3]

When things are going well, God often purposely fades into the background like white noise—barely recognizable but consistently present. Struggle opens up the possibility of an invasion of God's grace, a moment of rescue and redemption. Dan Allender describes the familiar, painful process:

> Our spiritual journey must lead through the desert or else our healing will be the product of our own will and wisdom. It is in the silence of the desert that we hear our dependence on noise. It is in the poverty of the desert that we see clearly our attachments to the trinkets and baubles we cling to for security and pleasure. The desert shatters the soul's arrogance and leaves body and soul crying out in thirst and hunger. In the desert we trust God or die.[4]

The problem is that this truth seems like nonsense while we're in the midst of our pain. God feels far, far away. We wonder if God is good, let alone present. But those who have suffered and come through the wilderness, Christians or not, often testify to a deep experience of grace: "It wasn't me. I'm not sure how I got through it, but someone was looking out for me."

God Wakes Us Up

If we're honest, we'll admit that sometimes we do need a wakeup call.

Shortly after the terrorist attacks of 9/11, a Rwandan student at the seminary where I was teaching pulled me aside. He was grieved by the attacks. Yet he was absolutely perplexed by the variety of superficial Christian responses he was hearing from pastors. He said to me, "These pastors do not know how to speak to suffering. They blame. They reason. But they do not look within."

I was interested in this student's response to suffering, coming as he did from a small East African nation that had been devastated by the 1994 genocide of nearly one million people. I asked him what he and others had learned from the genocide. To my great surprise, he said to me, "We woke up to our lack of reconciliation. We learned to repent. We learned to forgive."

Bishop John Ruchyana and his family fled to Uganda during the genocide, but quickly returned afterward to begin the process of reconciliation and restoration. Ruchyana says,

> It is wrong to say Rwanda was forgotten or hated by God. That is like saying God forgot Jesus when he was on the Cross. God does not flee when evil takes over a nation. He speaks to those who are still listening, He eases the pain of the suffering, and he saves those who can be saved.[5]

God was not far, he says, but near. As Ruchyana describes in great detail, Rwanda's great suffering awakened the nation to its deep divisions and its need for reconciliation. The divisions between Hutu and Tutsi, between religious leadership and political leadership, between colonial overlords and commoners all heated to a boiled point, manifesting in a gruesome holocaust. Rwandans had a choice. They could blame. Or they could begin to ask themselves difficult questions about these divisions.

Honest self-awareness at a personal and national level led to extraordinary acts of repentance and forgiveness. Instead of succumbing to its deep rifts, Rwanda emerged as a symbol of the cross and the resurrection. Ruchyana writes, "As a human being, to be able to repent of such demonic cruelty requires the cross of Jesus right in the middle of it."[6] Genocide awakened Rwanda and the world to the possibility of radical self-sacrifice, reconciliation, and forgiveness. That was the opportunity my Rwandan student felt pastors in the United States had missed in the wake of 9/11. As he later said to me, "Rwandans found evil within and confessed it. You looked for an evil enemy and attacked him."

While we may not comprehend the "why" of suffering, we can grasp its opportunity as a wake-up call. Says C. S. Lewis, "God whispers to us in our pleasures, speaks in our conscience, but shouts in our pains: it is His megaphone to rouse a deaf world."[7] National tragedies as well as personal difficulties offer us an opportunity to stop in our tracks and engage in an act of holy curiosity—What is God up to here?

I wouldn't pretend to understand why God would allow a terrorist attack or the systematic elimination of almost a million people of a different ethnicity. But I can understand the curious questions that emerge. I admire Bishop Ruchyana's ability to transcend the blame game and get to matters of the cross: repentance, forgiveness, reconciliation. I admire my student for challenging me to consider what deep work God might want to do in my soul, let alone a nation's soul. Yet I resist this holy curiosity. It's easier to resign myself to old patterns of blame. It's easier to shut myself off to opportunities for awakening.

The late Roman Catholic writer Anthony DeMello spoke often about opportunities for "awakening," as he called it. Much of his life's work was devoted to wake-up calls to Christians. He believed that most were sleepwalking through life. He wrote,

> Most people tell you they want to get out of kindergarten, but don't believe them. Don't believe them! All they want you to do is to mend their broken toys. "Give me back my family. Give me back my job. Give me back my money. Give me back my reputation, my success." This is what they want; they want their toys replaced. That's all. Even the best psychologist will tell you that . . . people don't really want to be cured. What they want is relief; a cure is painful.[8]

In my clinical work I've seen that people often don't want to look deeply within, to do the hard work, to wake up to the reality of their profound brokenness. Most often we try to manage pain.

Creative human beings have discovered hundreds of ways to numb themselves to reality. But sometimes the deluge of pain is so strong that we can't plug the dam of our grief any longer. In these moments, "relief" is no longer an option. A cure is necessary. We wake up to the reality that our ways of coping no longer work, and that we need repentance, forgiveness, and reconciliation. We hit bottom, only to recognize that our bottom was necessary for the kind of life God wanted to develop in us. In the words of eighteenth century Jesuit Jean Pierre de Caussade, "It is only when we have reached the bottom of the abyss of our nothingness and are firmly established there that we can walk before God in justice and truth."[9]

United with Jesus

The strange and paradoxical "gift" of suffering is little consolation to those who are in the midst of it. This is precisely why we don't "explain" suffering to someone going through it. Instead we sit with them, lament with them. We urge them to a holy honesty before God.

But those who have walked through "the valley of the shadow of death" experience a union with Jesus they can hardly explain. Somehow the husk of Christian rhetoric and doctrinal debate falls away to reveal the kernel, the significant core of our faith, the life of Jesus "hidden" in our own lives (Colossians 3:3).

A client of mine discovered this in and through a gruesome revelation in her own life. In her late thirties, Sue was enjoying a successful life as a lawyer and a mother. But Sue's well-managed world fell apart at a family reunion. The distinct smell of a particular cologne worn by her uncle triggered a flush of body memories, jolting her senses, turning her stomach, and scrambling her mind. Flashes of her uncle's body over hers ricocheted before her eyes. The smell, she said, seemed to "enter through my nose and rush through my entire body, infecting it with his perversion." She ran to the bathroom and vomited.

For the next three years Sue did the intense and agonizing work of therapy. In time, it fractured the family as Sue decided to bring out the truth to her uncle and to others in order to protect her children and others. Few members of her family believed her. Her vocational competence eroded and she was no longer able to compartmentalize her pain as she once had. Even her husband struggled to know how to love her and to cope with the new realities of a virtually nonexistent sexual relationship as she struggled to heal. Where was God? How could this be a wake-up call?

Sue remained angry at God for many, many months. She blamed God for not protecting her and raged at the disruption of her life and her family's unity. But her anger led to a growing sense not only of God's distance but of his care. "God became real, real quick," she told me. Moreover, she found herself awakened to her own spiritual and emotional lethargy. She'd been climbing the ladder of success but suffered a loss of closeness with her children. Her busyness also crowded out opportunities for deeper connection with her husband. Not only was God showing himself to be closer than expected, but her life was becoming more *alive,* as she'd often say.

Perhaps most significant was her growing sense of deep union with the crucified Messiah. Rephrasing Galatians 6:17, she said, "I bear in my body the sufferings of Jesus." She began to see that her own life—complete with humiliation, rejection, bodily harm, abuse, and a sense of God's absence—was caught up in Christ's life. Success was radically redefined. As an upwardly mobile lawyer, she used to see herself as invincible, even beyond suffering because of her tremendous resilience and adequacy. Suffering humbled her, exposing her true dependence, her neediness, her absolute inadequacy. Sue's life was transformed.

The apostle Paul talked about the Christian life as being "crucified with Christ" (Galatians 2:20), a necessary process for real growth to occur. Over the centuries saints and mystics have described the wilderness journey as "the way of purgation." That curious phrase conjures up unpleasant images, to be sure. Purging is a violent idea, an abnormality in the ordinary course of things—a stripping, a tearing, a pruning of all that is not truly us. It is a process that mimics the work of a sculptor. The great Michelangelo, when asked about his sculpture of David, noted, "I . . . carved until I set him free."[10] Beauty only emerges through the pain of carving, of stripping, of tearing, of pruning. The stripping sets us free to be who God made us to be.

Some find this idea offensive. I sometimes approach the board in class and draw a long line extending from the bottom left of the board to the top right. "This is the life you want," I'll say. "It's the life of upward mobility, of success." Then I'll erase the line, replacing it with a big "U." "The reality is that this is your life," I'll say. "The way down is the way up."

Theologian Michael Gorman calls this "the cruciform life"—meaning "conformity to the crucified Christ, a dynamic correspondence in daily life to the strange story of

Christ crucified as the primary way of experiencing the love and grace of God."[11] Sue, I believe, was experiencing cruciformity, a kind of union with Jesus that brought about radical transformation, and that could only have come through suffering.

When my class sees the big "U" on the board, I hear mixed reactions. Those who have experienced suffering immediately get it. They recall the Beatitudes and remember Jesus saying that the blessed and happy life is the life of spiritual poverty, mourning, hunger, and thirst. But others become defensive. "Are you saying God doesn't want us to be successful?" Or "Does this mean God wants everyone to be unhappy and to struggle?"

These are fair questions, particularly when we hear what seem like opposite ideas in Scripture. Jesus says, "I came that they may have life, and have it abundantly" (John 10:10). But ask those who are walking through the valley of the shadow of death and they'll tell you how they experience real "abundance." Most likely it isn't the successful or prosperous life. Nor is it an academic or professional achievement. Abundance, they'll say, feels more like a kind of intimacy and solidarity with the crucified Jesus that they had never before experienced.

For the Sake of Others

Letting ourselves be transformed by the cruciform way tends also to give us credibility with a watching world. As I talk to skeptics who question the veracity of Christianity, I find that most of them like Jesus quite a bit but are bothered by his followers. As a friend, a liberator, a healer, and a host to many different kinds of people, Jesus commands great respect and appeal. On the other hand, when these people hear angry rants against the very kinds of people Jesus embraced, they do not experience the welcome of Jesus. As one man recently said to me, "I feel like an outcast among Christians. I'm unclean. I'm not welcome."

When we follow Jesus on the wilderness journey, taking the way down, becoming conformed to his way and his character, we become healers who welcome the unclean and the outcast. Success is redefined as our identity emerges not in our ability to achieve self-sufficiency but in self-sacrificial surrender. Once again, the Exodus story reminds us of this lesson.

After God had rescued the Israelites from the horrors of slavery in Egypt, he called them to host and welcome foreigners, to look out for the vulnerable. What's more, failure of this basic hospitality would bring harsh consequences: "Do not mistreat or oppress a foreigner, for you were foreigners in Egypt. Do not take advantage of the widow or the fatherless. If you do and they cry out to me, I will certainly hear their cry" (Exodus 22:21-23, NIV). God recognized that Israel's suffering could lead either to bitterness and blame or to forgiveness and reconciliation. God invited the rescued to become rescuers, to extend to others the same grace they had received.

When suffering transforms us, we hunger for the same transformation in the lives of others. Shaped in the form of the cross, our sufferings lead us up and out into the lives of others, for the sake of the world's transformation. Isaiah envisions the wilderness as a place of suffering but also of redemption and fruitfulness: "Therefore I am now going to allure her;

I will lead her into the wilderness and speak tenderly to her. There I will give her back her vineyards, and will make the Valley of Achor a door of hope. There she will respond as in the days of her youth, as in the day she came up out of Egypt" (Hosea 2:14-15, NIV).

Speaking tenderly, God meets us in our moments of profound doubt, hopelessness, and uncertainty and invites us to believe that our best selves are shaped in the wilderness. In the wilderness, our selfish ambition is carved away so that we can love more faithfully. Our carefully constructed masks are torn off so that we can relate authentically and give freely. Our trauma is acknowledged and healed so that we can become healers to others. Eden's initial promise bursts into the pain of the present.

"The LORD will surely comfort Zion and will look with compassion on all her ruins; he will make her deserts like Eden, her wastelands like the garden" (Isaiah 51:3, NIV). This is the Exodus vision. The wilderness becomes a place of cruciform transformation, where our sufferings shape us into the kind of people God always intended for us to be.

Desert Drowning

My own big questions about the why of suffering began on a church retreat when I was just six or seven years old. As our group was enjoying a sunny afternoon of tubing down a lazy, upstate New York river, my ears were blistered by the screams of my best friend Robert's mother. Robert, a boy my age, had been sucked down into the vortex of a whirlpool. After a time, his body emerged. He was dead from drowning.

Drowning is yet another symbol used in the Exodus story to describe God's rescue. The Israelites went safely through the sea on dry ground, while the morning light revealed thousands of Egyptian bodies washed up in the returning waves. This event, along with the great flood in Genesis, fits a matrix of vivid biblical images for the transformative process of death and resurrection. It all comes together in the New Testament in the central act of Christian initiation—baptism.

Superficially, baptism and drowning seem poles apart. The first is a happy occasion, the second is tragic. The first brings joy, the second horror. Yet in speaking of baptism, the apostle Paul refers to the Exodus story, recalling that the Israelites "all passed through the sea. They were all baptized into Moses in the cloud and in the sea" (1 Corinthians 10:1-2, NIV).

Paul's cryptic words don't mean much until we probe a bit deeper. Ancient Near Eastern culture viewed water as destructive and chaotic, a force of death and evil. In creation, the waters are held back by the land and the firmament above. In the primeval flood story, the waters destroy the world. And yet, the apostle Peter reframes the event as a kind of cleansing or purging: "And baptism, which this prefigured, now saves you" (1 Peter 3:21). For Paul and Peter, the waters bring about life. According to Leonard VanderZee, "The drowning, destroying, chaotic waters become instruments for the deliverance of God's people."[12]

Drowning, this awful memory from my childhood, is the symbol of deliverance.

Early in my internship, I sought the advice of my counseling supervisor. A client was neck-deep in the tumultuous waters of sex addiction. Together we conceived of various strategies for him to avoid temptation and keep his head above water. It was the mid-1990s, and most of us knew little about the Internet or about ways to block or avoid porn sites. We'd talk about using the computer only when his wife was around, or removing the dial-up phone line to the computer when his wife wasn't home, even shutting down the circuit breaker. Both of us were working very hard to figure this out. And each week he'd come back having found some way around our strategy, feeling even more guilty and desperate.

My supervisor sensed my growing futility and desperation. She knew I had some lifeguard training in my past, and said, "Don't you know not to let a drowning man grab hold of you? You'll both drown." She had a point, but I didn't see it quite yet. Christians, I thought, were supposed to help other Christians stop sinning.

"Nothing we do is successful," I said. "He just wants to stop behaving this way. And my job is to help him."

"Then you've missed the point," said my supervisor. "Maturity is not about 'not sinning,' Chuck. Salvation comes through death. You need to stop playing your version of God and let him drown."

Let Him Drown

That goes against every instinct. I still find myself connecting with that feeling of being utterly perplexed by my supervisor's words many years ago. The basic human instinct is to help.

Parents of addicts will often tell you that they needed to withdraw their support and allow their son or daughter to finally hit bottom. Letting his or her child drown is a parent's worst nightmare, and it goes against every parental instinct. But rising up from the waters, the addict often emerges freed from the most destructive days of slavery. No doubt the battle with temptation continues. But many addicts find that after hitting bottom, the power of the addiction subsides greatly.

Again, I hear my client's question, "Why a wilderness?" And I wonder the same thing. Certainly, it helps to hear the stories of those who, like my client Sue, have braved the wilderness. But in the end, my eyes turn to the cross, where Jesus himself experienced the raging flood waters, ultimately succumbing to death. Robert's death—and all our "deaths"—are somehow caught up in Christ's death. And though I still struggle to understand why, I find myself comforted that the end of it all is not death but resurrection. After the wilderness comes the promised land.

And so I look back at this Puritan prayer, trusting in the paradoxical logic of the cross:

> Let me learn by paradox that the way down is the way up, that to be low is to be high, that the broken heart is the healed heart, that the contrite spirit is the rejoicing spirit, that the repenting soul is the victorious soul, that to have nothing is to possess all, that to bear the cross is to wear the crown, that to give is to receive, that the valley is the place of vision.[13]

Discussion

1. What does the idea of cruciformity mean to you? What would your reaction be to the big "U" on the board?

2. How does God draw near to those who suffer? What is your own experience of this?

3. Describe the tension in your own life of living in the way of the wilderness versus living to avoid it. Does the way of the wilderness mean intentionally choosing suffering? How?[14]

4. How does the Puritan prayer at the end of the chapter exemplify your life? How does it challenge you?

Part 4

*

Home:
Experiencing
New Identity
and Mission

Chapter 13

Open Hands

In order to arrive at possessing everything, desire to possess nothing.
—St. John of the Cross

It is a long spiritual journey of trust, for behind each fist another one is hiding, and sometimes the process seems endless. Much has happened in your life to make all those fists and at any hour of the day or night you might find yourself clenching your fists again out of fear.
—Henri Nouwen

***

"Just let go of it," my wife, Sara, told me one day as I was holding on to a grudge after an argument. I'd spent the better part of my day stewing: she was clearly wrong. I was clearly right. But she just couldn't see it. In telling me to let go of it, she was being downright patronizing.

First, I'm a therapist. I get what's going on, and no one tells me to let go of it. I'm the one who tells other people to let go of it. Second, and even more important, I *like* holding on to a grudge. When I know I'm right and Sara is wrong, holding a grudge feels good. It gives me a sense of power.

Like the Israelites, we can leave Egypt but it takes a long time for Egypt to leave us. We carry around our old hurts and resentments like weapons, ready and armed when our journey takes a difficult turn.

In conversations with men and women who have been betrayed or abused, I find that inviting them to let go of anger, for example, is like asking them to let go of a child or a limb or a precious possession. A woman who was abused as a child once told me, "Anger is the only thing I have. It's my power. It's my fuel. My abuser took everything else from me, but he can't take this."

When we've been hurt or when we feel insecure, the last thing we want to do is "let go."

How absurd it seems, then, when we consider the lofty ideals of Jesus, who presents "letting go" as the way to freedom: "If you wish to be perfect, go, sell your possessions" (Matthew 19:21). "Love your enemies and pray for those who persecute you" (5:44). He tells us to leave behind our old securities—and even our enemies.

The paradoxical vision of the good life envisioned by Jesus seems to intrude on our sense of personal power and even on the basic rights of life, liberty, and the pursuit of happiness. It challenges our sense of ownership. A recent incident with one of my daughters illustrates this. On a difficult day after Christmas, when all of the anticipation and emotion and energy came crashing down, Sara and I decided to take away our daughter's favorite Christmas present. In retrospect, it was a dumb idea. She was tired; so were we. But the fight she put up was extraordinary.

"This is not fair!" she yelled. "That present is mine. I own it. You gave it to me, and now it's mine and you can't take it away!"

I decided to push back. "Honey, you don't really own it. You can have it as long as we decide you can. It's ours." This was the classic dumb-parent response. You don't play lawyer with an eight-year-old.

"Daddy, that's so totally unfair," she shouted back. "It's mine, and that's all. You can pick from some other things to take away, but not that!"

Letting go? It's not so easy.

Clenched Fists

Henri Nouwen uses a compelling image to describe the difficult but necessary discipline of "letting go":

> A story about an elderly woman brought to a psychiatric center exemplifies this attitude. She was wild, swinging at everything in sight, and frightening everyone so much that the doctors had to take everything away from her. But there was one small coin which she gripped in her fist and would not give up. In fact, it took two people to pry open that clenched hand. It was as though she would lose her very self along with the coin. If they deprived her of that last possession, she would have nothing more and be nothing more. That was her fear.[1]

Nouwen proceeds to envision the human heart as a clenched fist, unable or perhaps unwilling to let go of something. Put yourself in the shoes of Israel in the wilderness, clinging with clenched fists to the old securities of Egypt, only to be continually disappointed. Imagine yourself having left so much behind, yet clinging to one or two remaining attachments from the old days. Memories of Egypt keep coming back, whispering familiar words.

It's a familiar and frustrating story. Consider the new mother who lost her own mother in childhood, and who has battled depression and anxiety her whole life. After her child is born, she falls back into an old pattern of binging and purging, putting herself and her child at risk. She and her therapist find that an old demon has reemerged—a deep insecurity that probably goes back to not having a mother, manifesting in an inner message she hears: "You'll fail at motherhood. You're already a failure."

Or consider the setbacks of a man whose parents were both addicts. "I was blessed with poor brain chemistry," he tells me, as we talk about yet another relapse. It's true. He was born at a disadvantage, and sometimes he finds it hard to believe that his luck will turn. Rejected by his fiancée, he finds that few others are willing to step into the minefield that is his life. "In the end," he says, "I go back to the bottle. In the end, it's my best and only friend."

Nouwen reminds us that the road is not easy: "It is a long spiritual journey of trust, for behind each fist another one is hiding, and sometimes the process seems endless. Much has happened in your life to make all those fists and at any hour of the day or night you might find yourself clenching your fists again out of fear"[2] Fear triggers the old clenching mechanism, something the Israelites could have related to. In the wilderness, fear abounds.

Although we wrap our clenched fists around all kinds of things—people and substances, money and sex—I often think that something else lurks beneath. It feeds on fear, taking over in times when insecurity and uncertainty abound. It's as old as the Garden of Eden and as present to you and me as our current clenched fist. The king of clenched fists is our need to control.

The story of our first parents sets the stage. In a garden that proclaimed freedom in every corner, humanity's first family saw only a limitation. The tree of the knowledge of good and evil was off limits. Why couldn't Adam and Eve take delight in the dominion they'd been given over all creatures and creation? This old story makes the point that even freedom requires boundaries.

Much like my daughter who'd lost the privilege of enjoying her Christmas gift, they cried, "No fair!" Because God is good, God gave humans the capacity and the good desire to rule, to exert power, to have dominion (Genesis 1:28). But this desire was twisted in the first moment of human pride as Adam and Eve wrapped their hands around the very thing they thought would give them control, certainty, knowledge, and power (3:6). We hit the replay button to this archetypal story over and over in our own stories each time we reach for the forbidden fruit, whatever that fruit is in our own unique story of rebellion.

We replay the story over and over again: in our attempts to manage our image, as we reach for yet another glass, as we click on a forbidden web page, as we hold on to the anger that keeps us from feeling helpless. We clench our fists because it's simply too hard to let go. Relinquishing control subjects us to chaotic forces both without and within ourselves. Though chaos is what we seek to avoid, chaos is what we get.

Control Problems

I'm not sure who came up with the term "white-knuckling," but it makes sense of this control dynamic. Picture it. In our attempts to manage away the pain of life and control our sense of freedom and destiny, we wrap our hands around what we think might help us. We grip the thing ever so tightly, so much so that our knuckles turn white, perhaps with fear. We cannot let go.

By the time Jesus arrived on the scene, the Israelites had become a fractured nation. When Joshua took the land, the hope that a life of shalom might abound was palpable. Canaan held the promises of a new Eden, a promised land full of joy and dignity and beauty and delight. But we know the rest of this story. Even in taking the land, the Israelites carried with them the tragic effects of the fall, manifested in their refusal to honor the boundaries of God's law. Control seemed a lot better than God's far-off promise of shalom.

In time, Israel demanded a king (1 Samuel 8)—a human king who could be manipulated, coerced, even bought. King Saul would reign selfishly, giving way to a king after God's own heart, David. King David himself would abuse his power, and King Solomon, his son, would follow David's lead. Solomon's attempts to control are documented in the book of Ecclesiastes, as it ruminates on the futility of control through sex, money, relationships, and even religion. In a generation, the nation would be divided into north and south, but that split had already happened in the hearts of God's people.

When Jesus arrived on the scene, Israel was a showcase of control strategies. The Pharisees had found identity (and control, to be sure) through the law. They had pitched their tents at Sinai, achieved control through dogmatic certainty and moralistic self-righteousness. They guarded Torah with a fierce resolve, because with it they would wield the sword of righteousness. The Sadducees, in contrast, sacrificed a bit of theological certainty for political savvy. They knew that real power and control can be found in bargaining, something we've since learned is a product of grief, not faith. The Jewish Zealots sought control not with political savvy or religious dogmatism but by the sword. They couldn't have cared less about rules or procedures. Their form of control came through might, and they would not rest until Rome fell. Trailing behind all of the others, quite intentionally, the Essenes maintained control through avoidance. Living in the desert under strict discipline, these men and women believed that God would find their form of control most worthy of appreciation.

Ironically, Jesus affirmed aspects of each control strategy. To the Pharisees he affirmed the law, noting that he had come to fulfill it (Matthew 5:17). To the Sadducees he affirmed political action, reminding them that Caesar was due his taxes (Mark 12:17). To the Zealots he affirmed righteous anger, turning over the tables in the temple (Matthew 21:12). And to the Essenes he affirmed separation, taking time away, retreating often even when there was work to be done (Luke 6:12).

But Jesus invited all of these groups to a faith that let go, a life with unclenched fists—and he sealed this call by his own example. Refusing to defend himself, he submitted to absolute vulnerability, hanging naked on a cross before his mocking accusers.

It's taken me forty years to become a master control freak, and I see the chaos it creates in every area of life: in my work, my relationships, my parenting, even in my prayer. With Nouwen I reflect, "I am so afraid to open my clenched fists! Who will I be when I have nothing left to hold on to?"[3] I've lived my life managing and maneuvering, trusting God only when I absolutely have to. It's a strange confession to make, particularly for someone who believes that God is sovereign. As we consider our own journeys, we may often find that our beliefs do not match the realities of our lives. Particularly as Christians we're faced with the painful truth about our lives. We're living contradictions.

What are your hands clenching? Are you the wife and mother whose husband has lost his job, leading to bankruptcy and the foreclosure of the home where you were raising your children? Are you the young Christian whose hands are clenched tightly around a need to be theologically correct? Are you the exhausted social worker whose identity is wrapped around helping people, even if your own emotional health is slipping away? Are you the lawyer who lives for the next argument, unable to relate in any way other than conflict? Are you the wife or husband whose very self-esteem is inextricably connected to your abuser? Are you the skeptic who can't relinquish control to a God you cannot manage?

Our forms of control are sometimes quite clear and at other times very subtle. Behind each is a good desire, a noble aspiration. But, like the people of Jesus' day, we turn the good things God gives us into weapons of control.

Dispossessed Desire

Christians are not Buddhists. We do not see desire itself as a problem. Instead we believe that our desires are good, but often misdirected.

I met with a group of pastors to speak on sex addiction about a year ago. Afterward, as many expressed appreciation, I noticed a lonely young pastor in the back of the room who didn't interact and left quietly when the seminar was over. Months later he phoned me. "Chuck, I'm a pervert," he said. "There is nothing good inside of me. I crave sex, and no amount of therapy or accountability or even meditating on Scripture seems to help."

I could hear him crying. These were the tears of a man who had forgotten his original identity as an imagebearer made for deep love and intimacy. As he told me more of his story, I learned that he'd first seen pornography at age eight. This early sexualization of intimacy had enslaved him to pornography, and though he'd left Egypt and was journeying toward freedom, he couldn't quite let go. His identity was inextricably attached to sex; his tears expressed feelings of utter futility and hopelessness.

He had been through counseling before, but it was pretty clear to me that he had received a message that is all too common and profoundly lacking. He had been reminded time and again that he was an idolater, and that freedom from his idol would come through repenting and believing the gospel. "I've just got to repent and believe," he'd say. "My repentance isn't deep enough, I guess." With every word, I heard more self-condemnation. It's not unusual for Christians to believe in grace and yet be masters of self-contempt.

"Women are beautiful," I said.

"Pardon me," he replied.

"They're beautiful. Sometimes I'll be walking down the street and see a beautiful woman, and it takes my breath away," I told him.

I wasn't sure if he'd hung up on me or was dumbfounded that a fellow pastor would say such things. But he stuck with me, and over the next hour we talked about his longings for beauty and intimacy and sexual connection. I couldn't see his face, but in his voice I could hear a sense of relief, of a burden being lifted. He'd spent years condemning himself as a pervert for being drawn to the very things God had created him for. To be sure, his desires had become possessive, misdirected, attached to pornographic images. But something inside was shifting as he began to dare to believe that he wasn't a "dirty rotten sinner." That day he heard, perhaps for the first time, that he was God's beloved, an imagebearer, loved and made to love, longing for good things.

Desire isn't the problem. It's possessive desire that is the problem. Gerard Loughlin makes this point persuasively his book *Alien Sex: The Body and Desire in Cinema and Theology*. He argues that growth and maturity do not require the elimi- nation of desire but the dispossession of it. Without using Nouwen's metaphor, he essentially paints the same picture. When our hands grip possessively, we're not free to enjoy the good thing God means for us to enjoy. Our search for pleasure turns into a slavery to it. Loughlin writes, "Dispossession is necessary for discipleship; without it, those who would follow will go astray. To love Jesus alone, as he wants, one must be free of all possessive relationships, free of the illusion that other people belong to you, are yours, extensions of yourself."[4]

This idea isn't new. Sixteenth century Carmelite mystic St. John of the Cross also demonstrates the paradox of desire: "In order to arrive at having pleasure in everything, desire to have pleasure in nothing. In order to arrive at possessing everything, desire to possess nothing. In order to arrive at being everything, desire to be nothing. In order to arrive at knowing everything, desire to know nothing."[5]

St. John is not condemning pleasure or knowledge or even reputation and influence. These are good desires created in every human being as God's imagebearer. But instead of opening our hands in a posture of dispossessive desire, we seek to contain it, to own it, to possess it. For that pastor who wrestled with addiction to pornography, desire wasn't the problem. In fact, it was the solution.

Dispossessive desire is desire rightly directed. It's a heart that releases its grip and relaxes into the deeper satisfaction of its ultimate longing. Matt Jenson, a theologian who writes on the subject of sin, writes, "Lest we should nudge a category like desire to the margins, consider the following words of St. Augustine: 'The whole life of a good Christian is a life of holy longing . . . that is, our life is to be exercised by longing.'"[6] It's a life lived open to the possibility of experiencing deep and profound tastes of that original Eden glory, but not to possess it.

Consider a couple who takes their honeymoon on the Caribbean island of St. Maarten. After a week of living in an exotic environment, swimming in tropical waters, and witnessing breathtaking sunsets, they return to their 800-square-foot apartment in an industrial northeastern city with its polluted air and low-paying jobs. After a taste of Eden, they find themselves right back in a barren wilderness. For the next week they make margaritas and play tropical music in their apartment. Eventually they begin searching online for a timeshare on St. Maarten. They decide to use a small inheritance to make a down payment and raise a glass to their purchase in paradise.

When they return a year later, the timeshare is a disappointment. It's not the beach hut where they stayed for their honeymoon. Nor are they newlyweds. An ongoing disagreement erupts into a full-blown fight on their first day back in paradise. They sleep in separate bedrooms for the first time in their marriage. This time there's no wedding gift cash to spend, so they eat at a roadside stand instead of a nice restaurant. The husband contracts food poisoning and is bedridden for the next two days. Paradise lost.

It happens to us all the time. We watch a movie that stirs our hearts and go back a second time only to feel a tinge of disappointment. We buy the car we've dreamed of only to wake up the next day with buyer's remorse. We return to the beach where we saw the perfect sunset only to find it cold and foggy. In other words, we feel desire, but in our attempt to possess it we experience disappointment, even loss. Dispossessive desire also leaves us with an ache. It does not bring endless satisfaction. But, as C. S. Lewis often reminded his readers, it gives us a taste, albeit a fleeting taste, of paradise, of shalom, of life as it was originally designed to be:[7]

> The books or the music in which we thought the beauty was located will betray us if we trust in them; it was not in them, it only came through them, and what came through them was longing. These things—the beauty, the memory of our past—are good images of what we really desire; but if they are mistaken for the thing itself, they turn into dumb idols, breaking the hearts of their worshipers. For they are not the thing itself; they are only the scent of a flower we have not found, the echo of a tune we have not heard, news from a country we have never visited.[8]

Dispossessed desire, it seems, requires us to appreciate all good things with open hands.

With Open Hands

Nouwen invites his readers to let go a bit more each day: "Each time you dare to let go and to surrender one of those many fears, your hand opens a little and your palms spread out in a gesture of receiving. You must be patient, of course, very patient until your hands are completely open."[9]

We know we are emerging from the wilderness when we experience a more continual, consistent freedom from the need to possess. The wilderness feels more like a battleground, while this stage of the journey feels more like the deep exhale after being underwater for a minute. No doubt old cravings will rise up, tugging at your heart for attention. But it becomes easier to say no. Having been refined in the wilderness, we know the geography of our addicted hearts, and we discover we're more able to slip past an old enemy.

But in order to live long in this land of unclenched freedom we need several things. First, we need others. The church becomes a place where we find fellow travelers attempting to live faithfully in the new land. In honest relationships, trusted friends who understand where we have come from remind us when we're clenching our fists. Second, we find that participating in the spiritual practices of the church strengthens us, reminding us of where hunger and thirst are truly satisfied. In my church, I open my hands to receive Holy Communion. It's a palpable reminder that in receiving from Christ, my heart remains open to its deepest source of satisfaction.

Finally, we become familiar with the roadmap, the biblical text, our script for living faithfully in a broken world. Its stories remind us that fellow pilgrims navigated the same roads. Knowing the rhythms of this story better equips us to live wisely in our day.

Living with dispossessed desire—that is, with open hands—is a gift, a grace, sometimes a momentary one. But after a long and difficult journey through a dark wilderness, each taste of the promised land is a welcome foretaste of the country we will someday call home.

Discussion

1. Not every metaphor works for everyone. How does the metaphor of open hands help you? If it does not, try to think of another one.

2. How might you be able to relate to the story of the man who lived with terrible self-contempt, believing himself to be no good? What good desires stand behind your own attachments and idols?

3. Nouwen says that many difficult things happen in life to form our clenched fists. What are some of the difficult things that make it hard for you to let go?

4. This chapter lists three practices that can help us live more faithfully. How have you experienced living with open hands in your own life?

Chapter 14

Restored Relationships

*I**t is not enough to leave Egypt, one must also enter the Promised Land.*   —*St. John Chrysostom*

Sin, both our own and that of others, drives us into customized selfishness. Separation from God becomes separation from neighbor. The same salvation that restores our relation with God reinstates us in the community of persons who live by faith. Every tendency to privatism and individualism distorts and falsifies the gospel.

—*Eugene Peterson*

Bit by bit . . . she had claimed herself. Freeing yourself was one thing; claiming ownership of that freed self was another.

—*Toni Morrison,* Beloved

***

San Francisco is a city you come to if you're leaving something behind and looking to find something else. It's populated with wanderers, seekers, pilgrims on a journey. Some of them wind up at City Church San Francisco where I serve.

Cheryl was one of them. She had lived in Los Angeles, trying to make it as an actress for a time. During the cold and foggy month of July, when most City Church attendees' pale complexions testify to a lack of sunshine, Cheryl arrived with bleached-blonde hair, as if she had just strolled in from a Southern California beach.

Over the coming weeks I discovered that Cheryl used to attend a church where she had dated a number of men. But she discovered that most of them, Christian or not, only used her. Until she met Ben. Ben was a community group leader, a single thirty-five-year-old. Cheryl was immediately attracted to him and quickly tried to make a connection. She was surprised when he didn't seem to reciprocate; naïvely, she wondered if he were gay. What Cheryl didn't consider was that Ben was more mature than the men she'd met in L.A.

Sadly, Cheryl hadn't known many men who valued women. Her father, a church elder, kept his stash of pornography in a place where he suspected no one would find it. Cheryl's mother didn't care, it seemed. She dared not challenge her husband's duplicity. Early on, Cheryl found that flirtation resulted in attention. She had sex for the first time at fifteen and never looked back. That is, until Ben came along.

Relationship That Redeems

For many of us, like Israel in the wilderness, life can be little more than survival—and living in survival mode does strange things to people. For many of us, difficult experiences in childhood lead us to compartmentalize the tough things while presenting to the world a more put-together persona. Some have called this the false self. We become the tough guy or the flirtatious girl. We assume the role of a devoted servant or simply become quiet and loyal. "To gain acceptance and approval," writes Brennan Manning, "the false self suppresses or camou-flages feelings, making emotional honesty impossible. Living out of the false self creates a compulsive desire to present a perfect image to the public so that everybody will admire us and nobody will know us."[1]

Cheryl's survival technique was wearing her false self, a glittering external image purchased from a plastic surgeon and a tanning salon. Meanwhile, inside, a series of soul-killing relationships confirmed one thing from her past: men are not to be trusted. Not even Cheryl realized that deep inside there was more to her.

I suspect that Israel emerged from Egypt self-protectively. After all, she'd been beaten up and kicked around by her old flame. Trusting Moses was tough, but, considering the options, perhaps the best thing. Even so, she'd hold her cards close to her chest and keep all of her options open—including returning to her abuser, Pharaoh himself. Israel's false self was tough and obstinate. She was determined to make sure that God knew that she had options (Exodus 16:3). And who could blame her? After all, Moses might betray her too.

What we discovered early on in our exploration of the Exodus story was that slavery ate away at Israel's sense of belonging and identity, causing her to forget her original story of beauty and dignity rooted in Eden. When difficult things happen to us early in our lives, this identity-killing process leads us to create new identities that protect us from further pain. Robert Mulholland writes,

> Our false self, having removed the roots of our iden-tity, meaning, value and purpose from loving union

with God, sinks those roots into multiple alternative soils where we seek to find our identity, meaning, value and purpose. Among such soils are our sexuality, our possessions, our status, our profession, our performances, our relationships, our woundedness, our resentments, our bitterness, our culture, our ethnicity, our place (geographical, emotional, psychological), our intellect, our education, ad infinitum. Our false self has constructed a complex nexus of soils in which the roots of our very being are grounded.[2]

To survive, we construct identities that suit us for a time, sometimes even for a lifetime. But occasionally someone who cares enough to peer behind the curtain intrudes, challenging our pretension and calling us to our true selves.

Cheryl discovered in Ben a man who wasn't willing to play the flirtation game. Ben treated Cheryl like every other member of the group, from the chubby forty-something who seemed terribly insecure to the software engineer and his flighty girlfriend. He engaged Cheryl as a whole person— someone who could answer some tough questions presented each week based on the sermon, someone who would pull her weight in the group, bringing wine and snacks, and serving every two months in one of the church's ministries.

The wilderness is a dark and lonely place. But relationship stirs in us the hope that we might actually become the person we were made to be. Cheryl began to see a healthy community at work: men and women, couple and singles, various races and classes, enjoying one another with no hidden agenda. It's the kind of community envisioned in the Garden, when humanity's first parents were bestowed with God's own image (Genesis 1:27)—the image of a trinitarian God, three-in-one, eternally in relationship. God's original design for self-giving love was embodied in this small group of men and women who would not ordinarily relate to one another in any other context. Quite unwittingly, Cheryl found herself caught up in its beautiful dance.

True Community, True Self

In Toni Morrison's masterpiece *Beloved*, Sethe remembers the twenty-eight days of freedom she experienced in Baby Suggs' Clearing, where a mix of preaching mingled with outbursts of laughter and tears brought a kind of collective purging, a taste of humanity amidst the brutality of her masters. That memory would allow Sethe to endure more hardship, yet with a new freedom despite the pain. Morrison writes, "Bit by bit . . . she had claimed herself. Freeing yourself was one thing; claiming ownership of that freed self was another."[3]

The great fourth-century Archbishop of Constantinople, John Chrystostom, wrote, "It is not enough to leave Egypt, one must also enter the Promised Land."[4] Entering the promised land, however, requires us to become unburdened, freed from the many false selves that hold us captive. While the wilderness exposes these false selves, it is difficult to live honestly, to live consistently, to live wholly. This is why we need community.

For *Beloved*'s Sethe, the taste of community was a reminder that slavery was not the final word about her. For Cheryl, the taste of community ignited hope that life and relationships could be different, that *she* could be different—freed from the part of her that needed to manipulate others in order to gain their approval. It would take time for her to "claim ownership of that freed self." But it was an honest conversation with Ben over coffee one night that would change her forever.

Cheryl had extended the invitation, writing in her email that she had a few questions about getting more involved at church. That was true enough, but Cheryl was more curious about this mysterious man who seemed indifferent to her flirtations. They talked about church and family and eventually relationships. After an hour or so, Ben needed to leave. It took several meetings and Ben's consistent curiosity, particularly about her family, for Cheryl to reveal the self she kept hidden behind the façade. But finally the moment came.

Ben listened as Cheryl told her story, weeping, hardly able to make eye contact. She talked about her father's duplicitous faith, her mother's apathy, and her own embarrassing choices along the way. This was new territory, promised land territory, a new geography of the spirit where Cheryl's image-management wouldn't be needed anymore. Cheryl wasn't sure how Ben would respond.

Ben asked her to look at him.

"Nice to meet you, finally," he said.

The song "Sigh No More" by the English folk band Mumford & Sons speaks to the reality of this breakthrough moment in our lives: "Love that will not betray you, dismay or enslave you/it will set you free/Be more like the man you were made to be/There is a design/an alignment to cry,/At my heart you see/the beauty of love as it was made to be."[5]

When we emerge from the cocoon that is our false self, we reveal to the world the beauty of our original design, tasting love as it was made to be. Because Ben was whole, having done battle with his own false selves, he was able to be a compassionate presence for Cheryl, a friend who would not take advantage of her. Ben's presence was the incarnation of Christ, the very presence of a God who "will not betray you, dismay or enslave you." Cheryl's relationship with Ben opened up the possibility that, in time, she might find safety in relationships with others, giving and receiving in community the way God intended.

Beginning with St. Augustine, theologians have understood that the human heart was made to live fully and freely in and for love and desire. The real obstacle to community is us—human beings living in a state of fearful self-protection. Theologians describe this with the phrase *homo incurvatus in se*, "humanity curved in on itself."[6] When we live a life marked by our old identities and false selves, we inevitably become hardened to others and resistant to love. We fail to live the life we were meant to live.

My grandmother was plagued by rheumatoid arthritis, an auto-immune disease that affects the joints. In her case, the joints became so swollen and gnarled that they began to turn inward. As her doctor explained, "Her body is literally attacking itself." This image describes life lived from the false self. Twisted and gnarled, these false selves barely resemble God's original design for us. Outwardly we may look presentable, but inside we're tormented, incapable of loving because we're incapable of being loved. We present only our false selves before God and others.

In honest community, however, we can participate as whole persons who are open to knowing and being known.

We can live out God's commands to love God and love our neighbors as ourselves. For that reason, argues Eugene Peterson, the historic phrase "There is no salvation outside of the church" is not just relevant today, but common sense. "Sin, both our own and that of others, drives us into customized selfishness. Separation from God becomes separation from neighbor. The same salvation that restores our relation with God reinstates us in the community of persons who live by faith. Every tendency to privatism and individualism distorts and falsifies the gospel."[7] In other words, when the church is really acting like the church, people may connect with honesty and vulnerability, freed from fear or shame.

Cheryl discovered that her father's brand of Christian faith was a twisted perversion of true community. The church of her childhood was not a place to experience God's presence in hospitality and reconciliation. It was not a place where confession was a regular part of worship, marking the community as broken and in need of restoration. It was not a place where men and women served alongside one another. Instead it was a place where Cheryl experienced the stares of older men at her teenage body, where women were second-class citizens, and where the message consistently seemed to point the finger at every other church for not really getting it. Like our first parents (Genesis 3:8), Cheryl hid—until she met Ben.

The Dance of Community

A few years back, I was asked to write a review of *The Shack*, a surprise bestselling novel that received as much high praise as it did utter condemnation.[8] My positive review ticked off more than a few students at the seminary where I was teaching. They believed the novel to be a modern-day exercise in trinitarian heresy. But I found in this story of God's trinitarian community modeling and extending compassion not only an important corrective to static representations of God, but an important message for some of my hurting clients.

Faced with an unspeakable personal tragedy, the abduction and murder of his beloved child, the book's main character, Mack, copes by numbing his pain, which he calls "The Great Sadness." He counters his pain with a "stoic and unfeeling faith." He quietly resents God's people and their "little religious social clubs" that "don't seem to make any difference or affect any real changes." He resents God's leather-bound book with its "gilt edges, or was that guilt edges?" He decides to deal with his tragedy through cynicism and resignation, a strategy many of us are all too familiar with.

One day Mack receives an invitation in the mail. It says simply, "It's been a while. I've missed you. I'll be at the shack next weekend if you want to get together. Papa." The shack is located deep in a frostbitten Oregon forest, miles away from civilization, the place where his great tragedy occurred. As Mack enters the shack, memories of the tragedy flood his mind. The sight of blood-stained fabric provokes a visceral lament: "Why, God? Why did you let this happen to my precious daughter? Why did you bring me here?"

Along comes "Papa." And before Mack's eyes a transformation occurs. The shack and its surroundings become Edenic. From the newness emerges a voice calling his name. A large black woman embraces him in a divine bear hug, "lifting him clear off his feet and spinning him around like a little child." Then a small Asian woman warmly greets him, followed by a strong carpenter. Mack is surrounded by a Trinity of affection. "Which one of you is God?" he asks. "I am," they reply in unison.

Mack's seminary training is no match for the wonders that follow. In the Trinity, he finds room for a full range of questions and emotions. Over the coming hours and days, he spends time with each of them. During his time with Sarayu, the Holy Spirit, he tends to a garden so chaotic and untamed that it makes Mack uneasy. Sarayu responds to his unease by saying, "Mackenzie . . . this garden is your soul. This mess is you. And it is wild and beautiful and perfectly in progress. To you it seems like a mess, but to me I see a perfect pattern emerging and growing and alive." Likewise, Mack's conversations with Jesus take place by a lake teaming with fish, a serene and beautiful place where Mack can lean into his strong elder brother with his toughest questions.

As I was enveloped in the narrative, I found myself appreciating Young's angle more and more. He wasn't attempting to write a theology textbook. Instead he was using a story to re-present the Trinity as a loving and safe community for the broken. In his unorthodox portrayal, Young understood something very fundamental and very important about the Trinity. He understood that the triune God—Father, Son, and Holy Spirit—is community as it is meant to be: its members giving and receiving, strong and vulnerable, leading and following.

This understanding of the Trinity goes back to the Cappadocian Fathers of the early church, whose very orthodox view of the Trinity emphasized the loving relationship between Father, Son, and Holy Spirit. The relationship was conceived as a kind of dance, evidenced in the theological language used:

periochoresis is the Greek word at the root of "choreography." We can think of Trinity as a perfect dance that becomes the paradigm for human community and relationships. Missional theologian Craig Van Gelder writes,

> God, in God's self, is a God in relationship. The Triune God moves together, creating a three-way circulation of love based on equality. Humankind, created in the image of God, is created with both a communal and sending nature, created for mutuality and interdependence, as well as for being open to the other. Christian community seeks to live with this periochoretic, relational identity and with this sending—for the sake of the world and for reality.[9]

It is this periochoretic reality that drew Cheryl deeper into the community of our church and her community group. Cheryl saw the dance, the beautiful interplay of men and women, of young and old, of different social and economic classes. She saw a mix of laughter and tears and witnessed both honest vulnerability and a willingness to serve others. And in her friendship with Ben, she received a palpable taste of Eden, a taste of love as it was meant to be.

Henri Nouwen writes, "When we honestly ask ourselves which person in our lives means the most to us, we often find that it is those who, instead of giving advice, solutions, or cures, have chosen rather to share our pain and touch our wounds with a warm and tender hand. The friend who can be silent with us in a moment of despair or confusion, who can stay with us in an hour of grief and bereavement, who can tolerate not knowing, not curing, not healing and face with us the reality of our powerlessness, that is a friend who cares."[10] For Cheryl, Ben and his small group became "the shack," the place where God's presence became real and tangible.

Exodus Relationships

During the long years in Egypt, Israel forgot about the covenant, that intimate relationship God had established with the patriarchs. But God "heard their groaning, and God remembered his covenant with Abraham, Isaac, and Jacob" (Exodus 2:24). Over time, Israel's sense of self had become intertwined with Egyptian life, where power, self-sufficiency, and self-protection ruled the day. Her habits and practices ran deep as a result of this long-term stay. So the journey out of Egypt was a mixed blessing: on the one hand, Israel was free of the tyranny of Pharaoh. But on the other, she was a long way from what God required in this covenant relationship.

Nevertheless, God was in it for the long haul, despite Israel's disobedience. God anticipated the difficulty Israel would have in this high-demand relationship, promising that a day would come when the people's hearts would open to God's love. No longer would their obedience emerge from a false sense of duty. No longer would they live halfheartedly: "The LORD your God will circumcise your heart and the heart of your descendants, so that you will love the LORD your God with all your heart and with all your soul, in order that you may live" (Deuteronomy 30:6).

That promise of new and open hearts has been fulfilled in Jesus Christ, the Son of God, God's true human covenant partner. At the center of Jesus' message was that ancient invitation, rooted in the original Edenic design for love and relationship: "You shall love the Lord your God with all your heart, and with all your soul, and with all your strength, and with all your mind; and your neighbor as yourself" (Luke 10:27). Emerging from Egypt, Israel wrestled with all kinds of self-protection and preservation strategies, but God's compassionate and relentless love would never fail (Exodus 34:6).

I often think of God's relentless compassion when I'm working with women who have been sexually abused. And I can't help but think of these many courageous women, who have journeyed out from Egypt, in and through the wilderness, and into life and relationship as it was meant to be. As a pastor and a therapist, I am privileged to walk alongside men and women who have experienced the soul-robbing betrayal of abuse—and to watch with joy as they cross the Jordan into the promised land.

Inevitably, what changes people's lives is not some concept or principle. It's not some bestselling self-help book or the memorizing of Scripture. Instead, what powerfully transforms, over and over again, is relationship. It's the presence of Jesus embodied in a friend, a therapist, a pastor, a group, in Christ's broken body shared in the Lord's Supper. It's a palpable taste of shalom.

It's the relationship that transforms.

Discussion

1. Perhaps you know a Cheryl in your own life. How do you relate to her?

2. How do suppose Cheryl's false self emerged? Can you identify how you too may have developed a false self? In what ways does that play out in your experience?

3. How do honest relationships begin to chip away at our false self? Have you experienced a community or relationship where this has happened for you?

4. How do relationships embody the presence of Christ? How is this happening in your own church?

Chapter 15

A Happy and Virtuous Life

Happy are they who, knowing that grace, can live in the world without being of it, who, by following Jesus Christ, are so assured of their heavenly citizenship that they are truly free to live their lives in this world.

—Dietrich Bonhoeffer

In the new heavens and new earth there is an entire way of life awaiting us, and we have the chance to learn, here and now, the character-skills we shall need for that new way of life— particularly the great three which Paul says will "abide" into God's future, namely faith, hope and especially love.

—N. T. Wright

A few months ago I met a student visiting San Francisco in his first trip over the Rocky Mountains. He really irritated me. He called me "Sir" and "Doctor" and "Reverend"—so much so that I made a sarcastic remark at one point. I found myself increasingly on edge throughout the day as he asked questions about the right Bible translations and appropriate dress for a worship service. It was a strange paradox. Here before me was a very nice young man, deferential and polite, the embodiment of Midwestern values. And he was driving me nuts.

I took a deep breath as I walked out onto the veranda connecting our church offices and did some personal inventory work. Was I mad at my wife? Was I stressed out at work? Was this guy triggering something else deeper inside me? To every question, the answer seemed to be no. I was doing pretty well, in general, even seeing a therapist weekly. Just then a colleague joined me for some fresh air.

"A great group, huh," he said.

"Really solid," I replied.

"I'm concerned about that young guy, though," my friend said, looking back over his shoulder to see if anyone else was around. "You know, the one who keeps plugging us with question after question."

"But he's such a nice guy," I said. "Look at him. He's the paragon of virtue."

"Chuck," my friend replied, "if that's Christian virtue, then I don't want to be a Christian."

In Search of Freedom

What is the happy life? What is the virtuous life? What does it mean to live faithfully in freedom and not as slaves?

For some, it's a matter of checking the right boxes—but many of the boxes have changed over the years. The virtuous life may no longer exclude dancing, or even drinking, but the litmus tests are still there, and they seem to be unique to each community of faith. I've lived in the South, where conservative politics and unspoken rules of politeness, combined with uneasiness about alcohol use, evolution in public schools, and celebrating Halloween, seem as alive as they ever were. In these contexts, virtue is defined by habits and practices that may not appear in any list of rules but seem to be known implicitly by everyone in the community.

I suspect that the student I met that day lived by his own implicit virtues—some set of beliefs and behaviors defining the good life that actually resulted in little happiness or true virtue. But was I any better? Just because I live in the "enlightened" city of San Francisco, perhaps the most progressive city in the United States, did I somehow "get" freedom more than this man?

I don't think so. I've lived in urban centers like New York, Chicago, and San Francisco, where a unique set of rules are as much a part of the fabric as mass transit and tall buildings. Urban centers are often known for their freedom of thought and tolerance for difference—but the implicit rules are just as rigid. In San Francisco, it's probably smart not to drive an SUV. It's not cool to eat at chain restaurants. It's a no-no to drink Starbucks coffee. San Franciscans typically have a bit of an urban swagger, a subtle elitism about coffee, wine, cuisine, clothing, and art. Litmus tests exist everywhere you go.

Freedom is an elusive reality. Try as you might, you cannot get away from rules, responsibilities, and requirements. A twenty-something who moves to San Francisco to get away from the stuffy fundamentalism of her small town might find freedom from certain rules, but will inevitably be sucked into the vortex of urban assumptions about authentic living. The upwardly mobile venture capitalist may gain wealth in order to give his family "the freedom they deserve," but will quickly find that this freedom brings yet a new set of required responsibilities and practices. You cannot find freedom without an assumption about the happy life, the virtuous life.

Think about it. How do you define happiness? I suspect your idea of happiness is inextricably interwoven into the assumptions of your subculture. For some, happiness is a bigger house. For others it is an organic, vegan diet. But freedom, at least the freedom God offers, invites us to envision a larger reality, a reality beyond the preferences of our subculture or the rules of our family system, beyond smaller forms of happiness and lesser forms of virtue. As N. T. Wright writes, people "who are called to be God's free and freedom-bringing people . . . must learn to live as God's free people, giving up the habit of slavery—yes, slavery is as much a habit of mind as a physical state—and learning the art of responsible, free living."[1] Slavery comes in many different forms, including forms of the happy and virtuous life dictated by our implicit virtues.

A happy and virtuous life, I would argue, is living and practicing God's future reality right now. This reality is set in the context of that first Exodus journey, with Jesus (Yeshua), the New Joshua, now leading the way. We are the New Israel, familiar not only with slavery but with difficult wilderness places, hopeful that God's promised land, "flowing with milk and honey," can break through into the present.

A life of virtue, of character, of mature and faithful living, can only be understood in light of this larger story of the Exodus. Jesus, the new Temple of God's presence, fills us with his Spirit and empowers us to live in responsible freedom as sons and daughters. Jesus is the new manna from heaven (John 6:33-35), satisfying our wilderness hunger. He is the living water that will quench the thirst of weary wilderness travelers (John 7:37-39). He has come to expose our lesser forms of freedom, happiness, and virtue, the ones that often manifest themselves in false selves and modest dreams of what we could be. He has come to invite us into a new and better future, right here and now.

To equip us for our wilderness sojourn today, Jesus gives us a new law, a new way of kingdom living that anticipates the soon-to-come future, the remade heavens and earth. To explore this new way of living we will attend to the words of Jesus in the Beatitudes (Matthew 5:1-12). When Jesus ascends the mountain to speak to his disciples, it's as if he is reenacting the journey Moses took up Mount Sinai. However, in his characteristically cruciform way, Jesus announces the kingdom by recasting the happy and virtuous life as a life of wilderness humility, of dispossessed desire, of costly compassion.

What we'll see is that the "happy life," this life of kingdom freedom, is not merely a freedom *from* slavery but a freedom *for* discipleship. And discipleship, as Dietrich Bonhoeffer reminds us, comes at a cost. Happiness is not a freedom from but a freedom for a life of love, a life of mission, a life of compassion. Happiness emerges from the recognition that God's grace not only frees us from Egypt but sends us into the wilderness to be released from our own attachments and to become agents of restoration for others. "Happy are they who, knowing that grace, can live in the world without being of it, who, by following Jesus Christ, are so assured of their heavenly citizenship that they are truly free to live their lives in this world."[2] It's this vision of the happy life that Jesus announced—not just for the first disciples, but for us today.

Happy Are the Broken

If we listen carefully to the Beatitudes through the lens of the Exodus journey, we may well hear Jesus saying, "I'm announcing to you the character of kingdom life beyond the confines of slavery in Egypt and self-salvation at Sinai." Knowing Israel's story well, Jesus offers a counter-vision, a transformative way of seeing ourselves, as well as our mission, while leaving the baggage of our old enslavements behind. He gives us a vision of the blessed life, that is, the happy life.[3]

Blessed are the poor in Spirit, Jesus says, for the kingdom of heaven belongs to them.

Blessed are the poor, the spiritually impoverished, the helpless, the beggars, those who are dependent. Jesus sees us at our most needy. It's common knowledge in the rehab world that addicts may need to hit bottom before they can discover freedom. Most parents know that some of the toughest and best lessons come when their children stumble and fall. We wish it could be different, of course. But as we've explored wilderness life, we've realized that its spiritual geography requires humiliation.

What's puzzling to us is that, according to Jesus, this is the road to happiness. It's utterly confusing for those of us raised in a culture where we feel entitled to happiness, a basic right of American society. Happy are the broken? This kingdom announcement sounds like a downer, the wisdom of a depressed Messiah. Parker Palmer, however, sees this wisdom as inherent to nature itself:

> The wilderness constantly reminds me that wholeness is not about perfection. I have been astonished to see how

nature uses devastation to stimulate new growth, slowly but persistently healing her own wounds. Wholeness does not mean perfection: it means embracing broken-ness as an integral part of life. Knowing this gives me hope that human wholeness—mine, yours, ours—need not be a utopian dream, if we can use devastation as a seedbed for new life.[4]

But I believe that this brokenness can also be misunder-stood. It has become a cliché among many who critique the ethic of success, particularly within Christian communities. In 2002 the late Mike Yaconelli wrote *Messy Spirituality*, a wonderful little book designed to invite stuffy, perfectionistic Christians into freedom.[5] Instead, a new generation picked up on this as an invitation to "be yourself"—warts and all. But what if "being true to ourselves" is actually an exercise in self-deceit? What if these selves to which we're supposed to be true are really false selves? For some people the mantra of "messy spirituality" took a direction Yaconelli didn't intend: it invited them out of moralistic and deadening ways of living but failed to cast the vision for the truly broken life as a mani-festation of God's kingdom.

Dominican priest and teacher Simon Tugwell summarizes this alternative vision of the broken, spiritually impoverished life:

Blessed are the poor in Spirit, those who have allowed themselves to be stripped of the old spirit, the spirit of acquisitiveness and security, because theirs is the kingdom of heaven, because they no longer seek to

possess but to be possessed, to lose themselves and all
that is "theirs" in the ecstasy of simple receiving and
simple giving again, or, more accurately, without even
any giving or receiving, in the simple being which is
the authentic image in us, that divine ecstasy of being
which is the living God.[6]

Tugwell's vision is of dispossession that, as we've seen,
requires us to be stripped of everything that vies for authority
in our hearts. It's a way of costly discipleship. A life of messy
spirituality, in other words, does not mean the freedom to
cuss, to drink, and to dance just because you weren't allowed
to when you were a kid. It's more than Celtic tattoos and nose
rings, just because you've been freed from the rigid standards
of Mom and Dad's faith. Brokenness strips us of everything
that is false in us, including the new personas we exchange for
the older, rigid ones. It manifests not necessarily in a more raw
or edgy ethos but in humility.

A few years back I got to know someone who loved to
drop the f-word in every possible context and every conceiv-
able syntactical usage. He especially saw it as his mission to
detonate an f-bomb in every fundamentalist conservative
Christian context he could. He talked often of Christian freedom and told many people about his struggles with drinking
and pornography. This friend had not yet discovered the brokenness and neediness Jesus envisions in Matthew 5. In his
insecurity, he continued to live out of a false self—this time
clothed in the persona of a radical, messy, "honest" Christian. He desperately needed to know that he was loved but

continued to manufacture affection in his life through this false persona. As Tugwell writes,

> Like runaway slaves, we either flee our own reality or manufacture a false self which is mostly admirable, mildly prepossessing, and superficially happy. We hide what we know or feel ourselves to be (which we assume to be unacceptable and unlovable) behind some kind of appearance which we hope will be more pleasing. We hide behind pretty faces which we put on for the benefit of our public. And in time we may even come to forget that we are hiding, and think that our assumed pretty face is what we really look like.[7]

When Jesus envisions the happy life as the life of spiritual poverty, helpless, and brokenness, he sees us stripped of every kind of persona, every manufactured form of righteousness or unrighteousness, everything that gets in the way of our flourishing.

The first four Beatitudes flesh out this vision of spiritual humiliation that leads to a life of happiness and virtue—a life of flourishing.

Happy Are Those Who Lament

In many ways, each remaining beatitude hearkens back to the first. Spiritual poverty undergirds each, because those who are not first broken lack the capacity to grieve fully and deeply.

Blessed are those who mourn, for they will be comforted.

Mourning, in the original language, imagines a kind of purging, a deep and guttural cry that exposes grief to the light of day. When we previously examined lament, we saw that this was very much a part of the language of the ancient Israelites, though it's not common today. The very idea that happiness might in some way be contingent on mourning seems odd and paradoxical to most of us. What could Jesus mean?

Once again, freedom comes at a cost. It requires every part of our being, every bit of the tarnished and tainted fabric of our souls. It moves us and shakes us to the core. Having spent many years around very intellectual Christians, I've often called this "the lost beatitude." When I was an ordained Presbyterian minister, I remember a pastor who wept often when he spoke in presbytery. A colleague said, "He's a 'touchy feely' pastor. No one respects him." That attitude is prevalent today, whether in the church, among tough blue-collar workers, or in the corporate world. A female executive recently told me that her success had required her to become tough, unemotional, in her words, "male." Yet, this beatitude reminds us that Jesus requires not invulnerable toughness but sensitivity, not passionless stoicism but deep empathy.

We are masters at compartmentalization. Robert Bly theorizes that from an early age we unconsciously cope with being born into an imperfect world by placing parts of ourselves into a bag. When Mom or Dad criticizes a behavior or an aspect of our personality, we tuck that part of ourselves away. We do the same when schoolmates laugh at us or mock us. Over the years, the bag becomes heavier, full of parts of us we're afraid to show. By midlife, it's a long, heavy bag full of disowned parts that need to be exposed to the light to be healed. But this exposure makes us vulnerable. It is often painful and almost inevitably is accompanied by a kind of grief for how we've lived, or how we've hurt others, or how we've hurt ourselves.[8]

I believe Bly is speaking about an opportunity for wilderness humiliation, blessed lament that emerges from a longing to live honestly before God and others. Just as Jesus welcomes orphans and widows, prostitutes and beggars, tax collectors and women, so he welcomes every broken part of us to the Table to be fed and to be comforted in a way that no possession, no relationship, no addiction can comfort us. Lament opens us to this welcome.

Happy Are the Meek

When I first really studied the Beatitudes years ago, I could not help but relate them to the grueling process going on in my own soul. Having returned from Oxford and started a degree in clinical counseling, I was being stripped of many things, not least of which was an intellectual arrogance. I wish I could say that this process was over, but it seems that I often wake up only to discover that I've barely left Egypt.

Blessed are the meek, for they will inherit the earth.

The meekness envisioned in this beatitude envisions an increasing humility of character. David Johnson takes this a step further, arguing that the word as it is used in the original Greek refers to the practice of "breaking" a horse.[9] A wild horse cannot be ridden, as its unpredictability and brute strength present a danger to its rider and all those around. A broken horse, on the other hand, is subject to its master. It does not lose strength in the process, but its strength becomes focused toward the rider's purpose. One of the goals of "brokenness" is this process of refinement, of repurposing, of refocusing.

The blessing, according to Jesus, is the inheritance of the earth. In Jesus' day there was no paradigm for brokenness, let alone meekness, as a means to power. Jesus transforms our understanding of real strength, exposing the futility of power through any means other than the humbling way of the Cross. The one who hung broken and helpless from the cross has been declared Lord of all. The victim is King.

Happy Are Those Who Hunger and Thirst in the Wilderness

For those who believe that faith in Jesus ought to bring complete satisfaction and continual happiness, this beatitude is a confusing anomaly. Didn't Jesus come to offer life abundantly, life to the full? Indeed he did. However, Jesus announces that satisfaction requires dissatisfaction, fullness requires emptiness, abundance requires insufficiency.

Blessed are those who hunger and thirst for righteousness, for they will be satisfied.

According to Jesus, a life of happiness and virtue requires a posture of empty-handedness. Jesus is calling us to a deep desire for righteousness, for God's kingdom. The difficulty is that our desires are misplaced, a problem that finds its origin in the Garden. As Tugwell writes, "What the serpent is offering is not something in itself wrong, then, it is rather a distortion in the mode of possessing something which is already there and which is good. It is a new concept of ownership that he is seeking to instill."[10]

Satisfaction, Jesus tells us, comes to those who hold out for the party in the end. Jesus is not envisioning a radical asceticism that denies any enjoyment of food or drink. That would be contrary to the life he lived. And it would miss the bigger point. As we've seen before, desire is not the problem. It is possession or ownership, as Tugwell insists, that gets us into trouble.

Perhaps Jesus is asking us to examine our hearts. Where are we grasping out of the need to possess? The invitation to hunger and thirst is an invitation to let go, to wait patiently, to find the greater satisfaction in allowing God to gift us with satisfaction rather than seeking to possess it on our own.

Happy Are the Compassionate

As a clinical supervisor in a counseling program, I found that students were always concerned that they couldn't counsel others while they were going through their own difficult personal process. Many were just beginning to deal with deep issues in their own lives. Often a student would walk into my office in tears before a session. "I can't possibly help my client tonight. I'm such a mess myself!"

Blessed are the merciful for they will be shown mercy.

To be sure, there are times when we need to step away from helping others for our own good as well as theirs. Times when our own pain overwhelms us to such an extent that extending compassion to another is impossible. Times when we need to step away for the sake of our own emotional and spiritual health. However, Jesus envisions a community where giving and receiving are active and inseparable, two sides of the same coin.

It's important to keep in mind what precedes the merciful life. In the first four beatitudes, Jesus envisions men and women who have been brought to the end of themselves, who have learned to mourn, who have been humbled, who have witnessed new desires for a righteous life growing within. Our movement outward—into the broken lives of others—is preceded by deep inward work. As a counselor, I've seen many people who live outwardly merciful lives but who are exhausted, burned out, resentful. More often than not, they have not been introduced to God's healing work in the first four beatitudes. Our own brokenness cultivates the soil in which a truly merciful life can blossom.

Happy Are the Pure

I'm a multitasker. As I write, I am also helping my daughters with homework. At the same time, I'm checking and responding to emails and monitoring Tweetdeck for interesting tweets.

Sometimes this gets me in trouble. My wife, Sara, can tell when I'm distracted. We can be out having dinner and she'll ask, "Where are you right now?" Her question will wake me from my wandering thoughts and I'll be back. Perhaps you'd call it double vision. Maybe this is what Jesus had in mind in this next beatitude:

Blessed are the pure in heart, for they will see God.

Purity of heart envisions a life that is single-minded in its focus. Ordinarily we are pulled in different directions. Part of me wants to immerse myself in a good book while another part of me knows that I ought to be reading to my daughter. Part of me wants to apologize to the person I hurt while another is whispering, "But Chuck, you know you're right."

The happy and virtuous life, according to Jesus, is the life of integrity, of consistency, of authenticity. A person with a pure heart is "a person of character consistency, a person who rings true whenever you tap her."[11] Having experienced the refinement of the wilderness, she knows herself and loves herself. As a result, she can love others with a purity of heart.

Perhaps the blessing of being able to "see God" offers us a single-minded focus, something those of us with wandering hearts and minds long for.

Happy Are the Peacemakers

A woman told me yesterday that she was the peacekeeper in her family. When I asked her to explain, she said, "I had the job of making sure my mom and dad were happy and didn't fight." I don't think this is what Jesus had in mind in this next beatitude:

Blessed are the peacemakers, for they will be called the children of God.

People often quote this verse in the service of conflict avoidance. However, the peace Jesus envisions here is shalom, the kind of transformative flourishing that comes neither through avoidance nor through power. It is the in-breaking of God's reign in reconciled relationships: when enemies become friends, Jews sit down with Gentiles, and Muslims fellowship with Christians. It's a woman finally bringing the truth to her abuser—not to destroy him but to save herself and perhaps him too. It's the kind of thing that can only happen if you're at peace with yourself. And this is why God runs us through the gauntlet of beatitudes—to prepare our hearts for the work of peacemaking.

As a therapist, I've often wondered if the blessing of becoming "children of God" in this beatitude is God's way of acknowledging how much we long for the consistent, compassionate, strong love of a Parent. The child of God does not have to appease God, avoid him, or work tirelessly to keep the peace. Instead, God's faithful commitment to bringing about peace in our hearts opens up the possibility for us to relax into the arms of the faithful, attentive, emotionally available Father. That love will propel us to move into the lives of others with the same invitation to God's shalom.

Happy Are the Harassed

The good life, it seems, is not Hallmark sweet. And so the culmination of these kingdom announcements seems, perhaps, the craziest of all.

Blessed are those who are persecuted for righteousness, for the kingdom of heaven belongs to them.

Being persecuted for righteousness is an inevitable byproduct of a life formed through the previous seven beatitudes. You see, a person who has matured in Christ's beatitude-way finds life's greatest satisfaction in taking up the cross and following Christ. As Christ's life is formed in us, we can't help but live more faithfully, more boldly.

A wise old missionary I knew once told me that he was scared to death of possible persecution when he first became a missionary. Back then he was young and arrogant, more devoted to becoming a "hero for Jesus," as he called it, than actually maturing and serving with humility. Though in his early days he lived out of fear and pride, age brought beatitude wisdom. He hit bottom and recognized his self-consumed ways. He grieved and he grew, and in time his life of service and mercy emerged from a new place of depth and humility. "The fear just dissipated in time," he told me, "and I longed to live as honestly, as boldly, and as lovingly as I could, even if it brought difficulty."

New Community, New Vocation

I've been around Christians who have a "get-saved-and-get-to-heaven" kind of theology. Anxiously awaiting the return of Jesus, they see little purpose in life other than getting others saved. However, the beatitudes invite us to see God's here-and-now mission. It's an invitation to life—to purpose in our vocations, to depth in our relationships, to risk in our mission.

How we live counts right now. "In the new heavens and new earth there is an entire way of life awaiting us," says N. T. Wright, "and we have the chance to learn, here and now, the character-skills we shall need for that new way of life—particularly the great three which Paul says will 'abide' into God's future, namely faith, hope and especially love."[12] It's fascinating to see that Jesus reenvisions our wilderness journey in and through the beatitudes, opening up for us the possibility of joining him in the cruciform adventure of becoming kingdom citizens, not merely wilderness wanderers.

In his exceptional theological commentary on Matthew, Stanley Hauerwas challenges American Christians, in particular, to see the beatitudes not as individual challenges, but as a communal invitation and announcement.[13] Christians cannot possibly live the beatitudes faithfully apart from the community of the church, the new Israel, sojourning today on its way to the promised land of the new heavens and the new earth (Hebrews 11). This requires the church today to become the embodiment of the beatitude vision. It calls us to become a community that demonstrates humble brokenness, honest lament, wise strength, faithful waiting, compassionate care, wholeness of heart, social and relational shalom, and risky engagement. In the life of the community, including the liturgical life of worship, we remember that we're the taken, the blessed, the broken, and the given.[14] David Jensen argues that as we are more deeply rooted in our Eucharistic identity as the taken, the blessed, the broken, and the given, we cannot help but see that our journey is not merely our journey, but exists for the life of the world.[15]

We enter into the wilderness restoration program exemplified in the beatitudes not for some personal enrichment program but for the sake of the world. As God changes us in and through the cruciform journey into brokenness, we emerge as people who can readily enter into the brokenness of others, who long to bring God's shalom even at personal risk to ourselves.

I'm struck not only by the implications of this for personal and communal life but for our work and play too. So much of the way we think about Christian engagement in our world is limited by behavioral approaches and slogans: be a good friend, share the gospel, don't cuss, be kind. Jesus invites us, however, to a whole new way of *being*, not merely behaving. The deep wilderness work exemplified in the beatitudes works itself out in habits and practices that cannot help but make us more whole, more human.

That was Israel's vocation too. As we've seen, we take our cues today from that tiny nation of misfits rescued out of slavery so long ago. Israel was marked by a covenant promise so that they would be a blessing to many nations (Genesis 12). But who knew it would happen this way? Who imagined that the journey would be marked by wilderness wanderings, glorious victories and great fortune, periods of intense suffering and exile, and return after return?

As God's covenant people today, we are participants in Israel's story. We are fellow wanderers through wilderness lands, breaking through to the promised land but often plagued by old memories of Egypt. God never gives up on us. He continues to remake our lives, casting the big vision for our maturity that we find in the beatitudes. The happy life, as we've seen, requires wilderness travel. But it launches us into new possibilities of growth, of service, of virtue, and of freedom.

Discussion

1. How does your Christian community typically define the happy or virtuous life? If you are new to Christianity, how have you typically seen Christians talking about it or living it out?

2. What do the Beatitudes invite you to in your own life? How might living into the new reality change the way you relate, the way you play, the way you work, and more?

3. Why does "beatitude life" require community?

Chapter 16

Theosis or Neurosis?

*N*euroses . . . *are the bonds that, though they restrict or enslave us, also secure our self-images in the world. As discomforting as they may be, we fear total disintegration if we were to let them go.* —Gerald May

To be like Christ crucified is to be both most godly and most human. —Michael Gorman

✳✳✳

I've often observed two pathways at work in the human heart. One is directed back toward Egypt, that place of emotional and spiritual enslavement, difficulty, and division. The other is directed toward Home—toward life with God. The former clogs the spiritual arteries of our heart, preventing us from living and loving; the latter invites God to do heart surgery, opening us to life as it was designed to be.

The first is characterized by *neurosis*—anxiety, depression, shame, addiction. Clients will say, "I just don't feel like myself." This is practically a definition of neurosis—we're not ourselves. Instead we're captured by some thought, emotion, or attachment that enslaves the heart, cutting off our connection to self, others, and God. All of us have experienced this in one way or another. It doesn't mean that we're crazy; it doesn't even necessarily mean that we need counseling. It means that we're in need of rescue, release, and redemption.

The second is characterized by *theosis*, an experience of deep connection and relationship as it was intended to be, a life of union and transcendence. That's what the apostle Paul was talking about when he said, "I have been crucified with Christ; and it is no longer I who live, but it is Christ who lives in me" (Galatians 2:19-20). Paul often talked of being "in Christ," a mystical union with God Christians throughout history have described in many different ways. This phenomenon has been called *union, participation, divinization, deification, christification,* and, especially among Orthodox Christians, *theosis*—"a state or process of participation in God."[1] No matter what we call it, it's an invitation to experience the spaciousness of our home in God.

Neurosis might be called the condition of the divided self. It's when we're not really ourselves, at least as we were meant to be. Our original design was for wholeness, unity, and harmony, both internally and externally. But as exemplified by Adam and Eve hiding in the Garden, we've engaged in theatrics. We've become masters at arranging our lives to hide the darkness and display our greatness. The great nineteenth-century preacher Charles Spurgeon characterized the phenomenon of the divided heart in a famous sermon: "Appear to be what thou art, tear off thy masks. The church was never meant to be a masquerade."[2]

I once talked to a man who had been "found out." His wife had walked in on him while he was looking at pornography, causing a collision of his squeaky-clean outer world with his dark inner world. Over and over again he'd say, "The guy looking at those images wasn't me. . . . I feel like I was taken over by evil." Truth be told, that squeaky-clean outer life was not him, either. Both were false selves, and it would take time for him not just to "feel like himself" but to experience the deeper and richer joy in union with God the apostle Paul was talking about.

While the wilderness exposes our false selves and divided hearts, we're invited into the new territory of Christ's life, that promised land of union and communion. God's Spirit invites us to find a welcome in the arms of a Savior who sees every part of who we are and loves us still. Christ offers us *ourselves*, purified through the wilderness and readied for love. No doubt we'll continue to revisit Egypt, revealing new layers of our inner resistance to God and to God's rule in our hearts. But gradually we'll see ourselves transformed, becoming more fully human. Becoming men and women who, in the words of Saint Irenaeus, glorify God by being fully alive.

Divided We Fall

One of the features of the early Christian community was the coming together in worship of diverse groups of people: men and women, slaves and free, Jews and Gentiles, rich and poor. Christ's invitation to be a body with many parts working in joyful collaboration remains, although the church has always struggled to live it out. Paul says, "For just as the body is one and has many members, and all the members of the body, though many, are one body, so it is with Christ. For in the one Spirit we were all baptized into one body—Jews or Greeks, slaves or free—and we were all made to drink of one Spirit" (1 Corinthians 12:12-13).

Fragmentation and division are the products of sin, the vandalism of life as it was meant to be. Sin divides us from God and from each other, and we hide. To be sure, our relationships are fractured. But we're also fractured within. Parts of us may go into hiding because the people closest to us won't offer the welcome of Christ to every part of us, and we feel unsafe. This lack of safety is not just something we experience in our workplaces or in relationships, but also in the church. As Spurgeon reminds us, the church would sometimes rather engage in a masquerade than live in reality. We live with divisions within and among ourselves.

To say, with Paul, "It's not me, but Christ in me," is to experience the welcome of Jesus in your life. No longer will you be satisfied with inner fragmentation. No longer will you settle for compartmentalization of your darker parts. No longer will you live neurotically, warring against yourself. Instead, you'll love yourself as Christ loves you. Theologian David Naugle affirms, "Not only is self-love scripturally approved; it is also the underlying premise of every blessing offered . . . in the Bible."[3]

I've heard a nasty twist on God's love perpetuated by preachers who seek to defend God's justice. They say that God cannot possibly look at a human being with love, but can only look at Jesus, whose sacrifice covers human sin and dirty, rotten sinners. But we may not allow theological gymnastics to cloud the basic message of the cross: God loves *you*. God welcomes *you*. True, God wants you to grow, to be stripped of false selves that hide from him and others, to be covered in the garments of a bride (Revelation 19). But God loves you in all of your brokenness, shame, and fragmentation.

I remember a church leader talking to my father when I was quite young about his particular church. This man said firmly, "We are the true church, the pure church." He had led the way through church divisions, expelling the "impure" from his fellowship. But purity, as we saw in the previous chapter, isn't conformity to a narrow set of rules. It is integrity. The pure heart is the undivided heart, the reconciled heart, the whole heart. If a church is to be pure, then, it is to be reconciled, free of division. Divisions are inevitable but are always grievous. In some cases people may need to leave the church or a relationship or a marriage. But this leaving is never the goal but an awful reality over which we can only lament.

In other words, neurosis is a cancer not only on the human psyche but on the church. It's a product of inner division manifesting itself in outer division. Theosis, on the other hand, embodied and incarnated within God's community, manifests itself in a life of self-love, self-sacrifice, and self-abandonment. It's the dance of God's Trinity lived among God's people. Neurosis drives us toward Egypt and a divided life; theosis invites us toward a life of unity and integrity in God. One destroys, the other enlivens. And, if we're honest with ourselves, we are always headed in one direction or another—in our hearts and in our relationships.

The Divided Heart

The divisions among us often emerge from inner divisions, from the stubborn refusal to allow Jesus to welcome every part of ourselves. I experienced this several years ago when my own inner divisions surged into conflict. I maintained my ground, but all along I felt as if something were really wrong—not necessarily with my thinking but with my being. I sensed that I might be right with regard to the principle at stake, but over time I realized that I was very wrong on a far more important level. I had projected my own issues onto someone I was called to love and respect. I had projected my inner divisions, my own need for *agreement* rather than *relationship*. The part of me that always needed to be right had not yet been fully crucified, humbled, reconciled within. I needed to be formed by more time in the wilderness.

Last year, while reading Martin Smith's *A Season for the Spirit* for my Lenten meditations, I found myself convicted yet again of my own wilderness ignorance. Smith writes,

> What chance is there of loving and respecting others if I refuse to meet and listen to the many sides of myself? How can I be a reconciler if I shut my ears to the unreconciled conflicts within myself? Now I begin to see that the spiritual life is based on a basic honesty which enables me to recognize that everything I find difficult to accept, bless, forgive, and appreciate in others is actually present within myself.[4]

In reality, we're often so busy that we fail to take the time to look within. We are more familiar with the lineup of television shows or the stats of our favorite sports stars or the status of our portfolios than we are with our own hearts. And this isn't merely a modern psychological critique. The great seventeenth-century pastor John Flavel wrote, "There are some people who have lived forty or fifty years in the world, and have had scarcely one hour's discourse with their own hearts. It is a hard thing to bring a man and himself together on such business; but saints know those soliloquies to be very salutary."[5] Knowing the territory of our own hearts is crucial for our successful journey.

God, it turns out, is far more familiar with our hearts than we are. Again, Smith writes,

> The Holy Spirit of God dwells in your heart and is no stranger to the diversity and conflict there. The Spirit of God dwells with and between and among all the selves of your self. There is no secret place where the Spirit has no access, nor any inner person excluded from the Spirit's presence.[6]

With God so committed to healing our hearts, why do we avoid the hard work of dealing with ourselves? Gerald May argues that our wilderness survival strategies work for us in the short run. They keep us together. They allow us to manage our chaotic worlds. And though they end up hurting us, the thought of letting go of that security is too much to bear. May writes, "Neuroses . . . are the bonds that, though they restrict or enslave us, also secure our self-images in the world. As discomforting as they may be, we fear total disintegration if we were to let them go."[7]

On our own spiritual journeys from Egypt to the promised land, we need to step into the fear May describes, the fear of disintegration that comes when we let go of the things that have worked for us over many years. They are like familiar old friends who have kept us company, and letting them go feels like risking our very sense of self.

While many people come into my counseling office to seek help for anxiety, depression, marriage problems, or anger, few actually count the cost of losing their neuroses. We'd rather take a pill than deal with the attachments that have been solidified through years of coping. As we begin to explore the core issues behind presenting symptoms, we find a reluctance to go any further. As one woman put it, "Perhaps I can live with a little depression."

Are we prepared to allow God to expose our inner divisions? Are we prepared to be found by God, to be incorporated into Christ's life, to find our identity in union with God? Though the answer to this question may be yes, living into that reality is usually much harder.

Receiving God's Welcome

Many of us have been fed with the husks of a false gospel that whispers in our ears, "God will love you when you clean up your act." Somehow, the message that God loves and welcomes us leaves us wondering if there is a catch. Or perhaps the thought that God could love *every part* of us is simply unbelievable.

Believing that God loves us as we are, in fact, may be the most daunting hurdle of the Christian journey. Somehow we think that we need to clean ourselves up for God, to hide our uglier parts and reveal only our glittering image. That's a false gospel. It tells us that God couldn't possibly look at us in our mess.

In his penetrating study *The Cross and the Prodigal*, New Testament scholar Ken Bailey turns the tables on the traditional reading of Luke 15, particularly the part about the prodigal's repentance (Luke 15:17-19). Bailey argues that even the prodigal's repentance was self-serving.

It's a familiar story. Determined to chart his own course, the younger of two sons takes his father's inheritance early and leaves home, only to squander the money on a lavish lifestyle. Life takes a turn for the worse, though, and the rebel finds himself penniless. Hungry and destitute, he finally smartens up. He decides to return to his father and say, "Father, I have sinned against heaven and before you."

The standard interpretation asserts that the prodigal son woke up to his bad behavior and repented of his sin, thus qualifying him for God's acceptance. But Bailey says it isn't so. Instead, he argues that the prodigal's confession is a ploy, a way of manipulating his father. In fact, this ploy was a feature of the Exodus story itself, with Pharaoh utilizing the same manipulative tactics. Wise to the mess he'd created, Pharaoh smartens up, deciding to make peace with Moses and God, saying, "I have sinned against the Lord your God and against you" (Exodus 10:16). According to Bailey, neither the prodigal son nor Pharaoh really meant it.[8] Both were ploys for favor rather than humble acts of contrition.

Instead Bailey argues that it's the father's welcome that changes the son's heart. It's the father's extravagant gestures of love that change him—running to the son as only a mother would do in that culture, extending compassion when justice was required, offering the best robe and the signet ring that would mark his identity as a son and not a slave, and throwing a party fit for kings and dignitaries. The extraordinary and prodigious grace of the father ignited the son's real change of heart.

Jesus is telling us that the father's humiliating act of welcome to this ordinarily unwelcome son is nothing less than Christ's own incarnation and self-sacrificial love. The story is not a nice little tale of fatherly forgiveness; it is the way Jesus conveys God's character and compassion. The powerful Greek word that signifies the father's compassion indicates far more than a change of mind. The father is moved in his inmost being, to his core. In that culture, Bailey says, that kind of raw emotion was only seen in women. But this is not feminization of God. Rather it is the humanization of God in Jesus.

It is the welcome that changes the younger son's heart.

The Father's love is unqualified, unconditional. You could even say it's downright foolish. Who in his right mind would give this son the keys to the kingdom, the signet ring? Only a lavishly loving God who knows us at our worst and at our best, who knows the whole story of our lives—and still embraces us.

The truly transforming character of this love is revealed when we begin to desire to be like that ourselves. I've mentioned that Roger was my clinical supervisor during a difficult and important time in my life. And I suspect that it was not Roger's wisdom or counsel that meant the most to me, but his welcome. He knew all about me. Sometimes I felt so ashamed that I wanted to sabotage the relationship before Roger could reject me. I remember cancelling one week, feeling sick, not physically but *cynically* sick, convinced that this kind of unconditional welcome was not possible. But Roger called that week to check in on me. His compassion instilled in me a deep desire to be a more fully human person, undivided, compassionate, whole.

In an even more profound way, God's unconditional welcome invites us to bring our whole selves into his compassionate embrace.

Home Sweet Home

Many of us are infected with a kind of Christian Platonism that denigrates the *merely* human. To be godly, we think, means somehow transcending "the flesh," overcoming the body, becoming more spiritual or holy. Yet Jesus became human precisely to affirm and redeem our humanity, to remake us, to restore us to our original design and more. "To be like Christ crucified," writes theologian Michael Gorman, "is to be both most godly and most human."[9]

It's the part about being human that makes us stumble, of course.

Yet the goal of this Exodus journey and the reason why we've persevered is not, in the end, to be divided yet again, with all of our brokenness cast away. The goal is to be remade, restored, renewed, made whole. The promised land envisioned in Revelation 21 is a new earth, where a new humanity lives, once and for all, into the great vision of *shalom*—peace, reconciliation, relational unity, healing, flourishing, and so much more.[10] Robert Webber articulates this reality:

> Since God has already accepted us in Christ, who lifted our humanity up into his, and by the Spirit has done everything necessary to make us acceptable

to God, the spiritual life is a freedom to participate in God, not a duty. In Jesus, we are born again to become fully human, to be what God created us to be in the first place. So the spiritual life, this marriage we have with God, is an embodied union with God and with his vision for the world revealed to us in Jesus by the Spirit. Our spiritual life, then, is not just a feeling, an idea, or a spiritual romance. No! It is an embodiment of God's vision for humanity clearly spoken in the words of Jesus and visualized in concrete ways in his actions.[11]

Home, then, is not just where the heart is, or where a disembodied soul ends up. It's where we find our life fully formed as human beings. God invites us by his Spirit to anticipate this future right now as we begin to taste this human flourishing in every way—relationally, socially, physically, emotionally, spiritually—all "new creation" life (2 Corinthians 5:17).

Neurosis leads us back to Egypt, back to relationships and addictions and emotions and attitudes that offer a taste of satisfaction but ultimately disappoint. Theosis draws us up and out, beyond our false selves and into our full humanity.

Neurosis is tangled up in a false gospel of image and appearance, where God waits for us to tidy ourselves up before welcoming us. Theosis invites us to recognize God running toward us, ready to welcome us, brokenness and all.

Neurosis tells us that our humanity is a problem, that our bodies just get us into trouble, and that real maturity manifests in a kind of hyperspiritual "über-saint." Theosis reminds us that God isn't afraid of us; God's Spirit dwells in us in order to make us fully human.

Much of what we call North American Christianity is entrenched in the trajectory of neurosis, leading to spiritual burnout, emotional exhaustion, and a faith that makes little sense to a watching world—a world that sees our hypocrisy better than we do.

Home isn't a place where we have to put on appearances. Home is a place where God smiles on us, dwells in us, and embraces us. That's the real "home, sweet home."

In the End Is Our Beginning

Our journey together began with a story I told about Professor Alister McGrath, a theologian who opened my eyes to the many ways in which the Exodus story maps our human journey.

When Professor McGrath first told our class about this great Exodus journey we're on, my first reaction was a rush of shame. Growing up in a context where I always felt as if I wasn't living up to God's high standards, I took McGrath's teaching as a reminder of how badly I'd fumbled the journey. It seemed to me that my Egypts were so powerful and so innumerable that I'd never make much progress along this Exodus way.

But the further we entered into the story, the more it came to feel like an invigorating shower of water on a scorching desert day. Yes, we have fumbled on the journey and we will continue to fumble along the way. God's chosen band of misfits get themselves into trouble time and again. Yet the more we veer off course, the closer God wants to draw near.

God keeps accompanying us along the way: back then in a cloud, in a prophet, in manna, in a tent; and now in Jesus and, even more intimately, in the Spirit. As we wander, God just draws closer, not further away.

This past year I turned forty. I thought I would have figured out more than I have already. If someone were to plot my course to this point, it would be a jagged line, certainly too jagged, some might say, to be a pastor, a professor, or a counselor. But with each dead end and each wrong turn, I'm learning to listen to God's Spirit whispering, "Chuck, let me drive. Just get a little rest." Still reluctant, my hands grip the wheel, but more lightly by the day.

I tune in to that ancient voice of the prophet Isaiah: "In the wilderness prepare the way for the LORD; make straight in the desert a highway for our God. Every valley shall be raised up, every mountain and hill made low; the rough ground shall become level, the rugged places a plain" (Isaiah 40:3-4, NIV).

And I keep moving, trusting more and more in the Spirit to keep me on that highway.

Discussion

1. What is neurosis? Think of a time when it felt as if someone else were living your life.

2. What is theosis? Think of a time when it felt as if God were showing up in and through you, so that you could identify with the apostle Paul, saying, "It's not me, it's Christ in me."

3. How does the choice between neurosis and theosis define your life? Where are you in the journey right now?

4. What does Luke 15 and the story of God's welcome teach you?

5. What would it mean to receive God's welcome? How have you sabotaged it? How would you like to receive it?

Notes

Introduction

1. Alister McGrath, *The Journey: A Pilgrim in the Lands of the Spirit* (New York: G. K. Hall, 2000), p. 23.

Chapter 1

1. C. S. Lewis, *The Weight of Glory* (New York: HarperOne, 2001), p. 30.

2. Estelle Frankel, *Sacred Therapy: Jewish Spiritual Teachings on Inner Healing and Emotional Wholeness* (Boston: Shambhala, 2005), p. 103.

3. Gerald May, *The Awakened Heart* (New York: HarperOne, 1993), p. 1.

4. Henri Nouwen, *The Return of the Prodigal Son* (New York: Image/Doubleday, 1994), p. 107.

5. G. K. Chesterton, *Orthodoxy: The Romance of Faith* (New York: Doubleday, 1990), p. 54.

6. *The Shawshank Redemption*, dir. Frank Darabont, Castle Rock Entertainment, Burbank, 1994.

7. C. S. Lewis, *The Screwtape Letters* (New York: HarperCollins, 2001), p. 44.

Chapter 2

1. Walter Brueggemann, *The Psalms and the Life of Faith* (Minneapolis, Minn.: Fortress, 1995), p. 68.
2. Thomas Merton, *Conjectures of a Guilty Bystander* (New York: Image/Doubleday, 1968), p. 86.
3. David Whyte, *The Three Marriages: Reimaging Work, Self, and Relationship* (New York: Riverhead/Penguin, 2009), p. 113.
4. William Cope Moyers, *Broken: My Story of Addiction and Redemption* (New York: Viking/Penguin, 2006), p. 133.
5. Gerald May, *Addiction and Grace* (New York: Harper-One, 1991), p. 3.
6. May, *Addiction and Grace*, p. 14.

Chapter 3

1. Teresa of Avila, *The Interior Castle* (Mahwah, N.J.: Paulist Press, 1979), p. 51.
2. *The Shawshank Redemption*

Chapter 4

1. Gordon Dalbey, *Healing the Masculine Soul* (Nashville: Thomas Nelson, 2004), p. xvi.
2. Irwin Kula, *Yearnings: Embracing the Sacred Messiness of Life* (New York: Hyperion, 2006), p. 111.
3. G. K. Chesterton, *What I Saw in America* (Middlesex: Echo Library, 2009), p. 94.
4. Dietrich Bonhoeffer, *Life Together: The Classic Exploration of Faith in Community* (New York: HarperOne, 1978), p. 119.

5. Brian Walsh and Sylvia Keesmaat, *Colossians Remixed* (Downers Grove, Ill.: InterVarsity, 2004), p. 110.
6. Brennan Manning, *Ruthless Trust* (New York: Harper Collins, 2002), p. 12.

Chapter 5

1. Nicolas Berdyaev, *Slavery and Freedom* (San Rafael: Semantron Press, 2009), p. 247.
2. Jacob Neusner, *Three Questions of Formative Judaism: History, Literature, and Religion* (Boston: Brill Academic, 2002), p. 83.

Chapter 6

1. Dan Allender, *Bold Love* (Colorado Springs: NavPress, 1992), p. 28.
2. Henri Nouwen, *The Way of the Heart* (New York: Harper Collins, 1991), p. 34.
3. Allender, *Bold Love*, p. 19.
4. Thomas Merton, *No Man Is an Island* (Boston: Shmbhala, 1955), p. xxi.

Chapter 7

1. Commentator Peter Enns says that the phrase "this fellow Moses" conveys a sense of contempt and derision in both the original Hebrew and English, a kind of contempt familiar to an angry child whose parents are delayed in picking him up. See Enns, *Exodus: The NIV Application Commentary* (Grand Rapids, Mich.: Zondervan, 2000), p. 569.

2. Henri Nouwen, *Life of the Beloved* (New York: Crossway, 1992), p. 21.

3. Gerald May, *Addiction and Grace*, p. 90.

Chapter 8

1. Paul David Tripp, *Whiter Than Snow* (Wheaton, Ill.: Crossway Books, 2008), p. 32.

2. C. S. Lewis, *The Problem of Pain* (New York: Harper Collins, 2001), p. 88.

3. Stephen Dempster, *Dominion and Dynasty* (Downers Grove, Ill.: InterVarsity, 2003), p. 101.

4. From Ernst Kurtz and Elizabeth Ketcham, *The Spirituality of Imperfection* (New York: Bantam, 1992), p. 49.

5. Dan Allender, *The Wounded Heart* (Colorado Springs: NavPress, 1990), p. 58.

6. Viktor Frankl, *Man's Search for Meaning* (Boston: Beacon, 1992), p. 75.

Chapter 9

1. Quoted in Parker J. Palmer, *A Hidden Wholeness* (Hoboken: Jossey-Bass, 2009), p. 181.

2. Dempster, *Dominion and Dynasty*, p. 11.

Chapter 10

1. Dan Allender, "The Hidden Hope in Lament," *Mars Hill Review*, 1994, www.leaderu.com/marshill/mhr01/lament1.html.

2. Parker Palmer, *The Politics of the Brokenhearted* (Kalamazoo: Fetzer Institute, 2005), p. 246.

3. See Peterson's discussion of the book of Lamentations in *Five Smooth Stones for Pastoral Work* (Grand Rapids, Mich.: Eerdmans, 1992), pp. 113-145.

4. David Benner, *Care of Souls: Revisioning Christian Nurture and Counsel* (Grand Rapids, Mich.: Baker, 1998), p. 36.

5. John Goldingay, *Walk On: Life, Loss, Trust, and Other Realities* (Grand Rapids, Mich.: Baker Academic, 2002), p. 97.

Chapter 11

1. Raymond Brown, *The Message of Numbers* (Downers Grove, Ill.: InterVarsity, 2002), p. 119.

2. David Stubbs, *Numbers* (Grand Rapids, Mich.: Brazos, 2009), p. 128.

3. Ibid., p. 130.

4. Brown, *The Message of Numbers*, p. 119.

5. Stubbs, *Numbers*, p. 131.

6. From Michael Ford, *The Wounded Prophet* (New York: Image, 2002), p. 116.

7. Timothy Jones, *Awake My Soul: Practical Spirituality for Busy People* (New York, Doubleday, 1999), p. 88.

8. John Calvin, *Institutes of the Christian Religion*, 3.6.5.

9. George McDonald, *Diary of an Old Soul* (London: Longmans, Green & Co., 1885), p. 11.

10. Frederick Buechner, *Telling Secrets* (New York: HarperCollins, 1991), p. 32.

Chapter 12

1. N. T. Wright, "A Royal Priesthood: The Use of the Bible Ethically and Politically," www.ntwrightpage.com/Wright_Paul_Caesar_Romans.htm.

2. Timothy Keller from a sermon called "The Lord of Salvation" at http://sermons.redeemer.com/store/index.cfm?fuseaction=product.display&Product_ID=18094.

3. Vaclev Havel, *The Art of the Impossible: Politics as Morality in Practice* (New York: Knopf, 1997), p. 54.

4. Dan Allender, *The Healing Path* (Colorado Springs: Waterbrook Press, 2000), p. 21.

5. John Ruchyana, *The Bishop of Rwanda* (Nashville: Thomas Nelson, 2007), p. xv.

6. Ibid., p. 96.

7. C. S. Lewis, *The Problem of Pain* (New York: Harper Collins, 2001), p. 91.

8. Anthony DeMello, "Relief Not Cure," Oct. 6, 2003, at www.ijourney.org/index.php?tid=301.

9. Jean Pierre de Caussade, www.mountainrunnerdoc.com/JPdeCaussade.html.

10. J. Patrick Lewis, *Michelangelo's World* (Mankato, Minn.: Creative Editions, 2007), p. 7.

11. Michel Gorman, *Cruciformity: Paul's Narrative Spirituality of the Cross* (Grand Rapids, Mich.: Eerdmans, 2001), p. 5.

12. Leonard VanderZee, *Christ, Baptism, and the Lord's Supper* (Downers Grove, Ill.: IVP Academic, 2004), p. 75.

13. www.oldlandmarks.com/puritan.htm#The%20Valley%20of%20Vision.

14. I have written on this, particularly as it relates to situations of abuse. It is important for those who are abused to see that God does not want them to stay in an abusive relationship just to experience growth in character. This is a misunderstanding of the wilderness way. See www.drchuckdegroat. com/2009/05/identity-abuse-and-cruciformity-does-being-like-jesus-mean-staying-with-an-abuser/.

Chapter 13

1. Henri Nouwen, *With Open Hands* (Notre Dame: Ave Maria, 2005), p. 20.
2. Ibid., p. 26.
3. Ibid., p. 27.
4. Gerard Loughlin, *Alien Sex: The Body and Desire in Cinema and Theology* (Malden, Mass.: Blackwell, 2004), p. 18.
5. John of the Cross, *Ascent of Mt. Carmel*, trans. E. Allison Peers (Radford, Vir.: Wilder, 2008), p. 108.
6. Matt Jenson, *Gravity of Sin* (New York: T&T Clark, 2006), p. 25.
7. For more on this central theme in C. S. Lewis, see Corbin Scott Carnell, *Bright Shadow of Reality: Spiritual Longing in C. S. Lewis* (Grand Rapids, Mich.: Eerdmans, 1999).
8. Lewis, *The Weight of Glory*, p. 90.
9. Nouwen, *With Open Hands*, p. 25.

Chapter 14

1. Brennan Manning, *Abba's Child* (Colorado Springs, NavPress, 2002), p. 34.

2. Robert Mulholland, *The Deeper Journey* (Downers Grove, Ill.: InterVarsity, 2006), p. iii.

3. Toni Morrison, *Beloved* (New York: Knopf, 2006), p. 112.

4. Cited in Thomas Merton, *Contemplative Prayer* (New York: Image, 1996), p. 60.

5. Marcus Mumford, "Sigh No More," *Sigh No More*, © 2009 Universal Music.

6. For a thorough analysis of this idea, see Jenson, *Gravity of Sin*.

7. Eugene Peterson, *Reversed Thunder* (New York: Harper Collins, 1988), p. 43.

8. William Young, *The Shack* (Newbury Park, Calif.: Windblown Media, 2007).

9. Craig Van Gelder, *The Missional Church and Leadership Formation* (Grand Rapids, Mich.: Eerdmans, 2009), p. 197.

10. Henri Nouwen, *Out of Solitude* (Notre Dame: Ave Maria, 1974), p. 34.

Chapter 15

1. N. T. Wright, *After You Believe: Why Christian Character Matters* (New York: Harper Collins, 2010), p. 92.

2. Dietrich Bonhoeffer, *The Cost of Discipleship* (New York: Touchstone, 1995), p. 56.

3. The "blessed" or "happy" (μακαριοσ) life is a life of fullness, flourishing, envisioning God's shalom.

4. Parker Palmer, *A Hidden Wholeness* (San Francisco: Jossey Bass, 2004), p. 5.

5. Michael Yaconelli, *Messy Spirituality* (Grand Rapids, Mich.: Zondervan, 2002).

6. Simon Tugwell, *The Beatitudes: Soundings in Christian Traditions* (Springfield, Ill.: Templegate, 1980), p. 28.

7. Ibid., p. 130.

8. See an online version of Bly's work on the "long bag we drag behind us" at www.mfarnworth.com/360Readings/TheLongBag.htm.

9. David Johnson, *Joy Comes in the Mourning* (Camp Hill, Penn.: Christian Publications, 1998).

10. Tugwell, *Beatitudes*, p. 22.

11. Cornelius Plantinga, *Not the Way It's Supposed to Be: A Breviary of Sin* (Grand Rapids, Mich.: Eerdmans, 1995), p. 35.

12. "The Rebirth of Virtue: An Interview with Tom Wright," at http://trevinwax.com/2010/01/05/the-rebirth-of-virtue-an-interview-with-n-t-wright/.

13. Stanley Hauerwas, *Matthew* (Grand Rapids, Mich.: Brazos 2007), p. 51.

14. My colleague at Newbigin House, Dr. Scot Sherman, elaborates on this in a forthcoming book on liturgy and mission. He shows how the church, in its liturgical life, lives out the cruciform vision we've explored.

15. For an elaboration on this theme, see chapter 4, David Jensen, *Responsive Labor: A Theology of Work* (Louisville: John Knox, 2006).

Chapter 16

1. Robert Webber, *The Divine Embrace* (Grand Rapids, Mich.: Eerdmans, 2006), p. 41.
2. Charles Spurgeon, "A Divided Heart," www.spurgeon.org/sermons/0276.htm.
3. David K. Naugle, *Reordered Love, Reordered Lives: Learning the Deep Meaning of Happiness* (Grand Rapids, Mich.: Eerdmans, 2008), p. 101.
4. Martin Smith, *A Season for the Spirit* (New York: Seabury, 2004), p. 36.
5. John Flavel, *Keeping the Heart* (ReadaClassic.com, 2010), p. 8.
6. Smith, *A Season for the Spirit*, p. 35.
7. Gerald May, *Will and Spirit: A Contemplative Psychology* (New York: Harper Collins, 1982), pp. 226-227.
8. Kenneth Bailey, *The Cross and the Prodigal* (Downers Grove, Ill.: InterVarsity, 2006), pp. 59-60.
9. Michael Gorman, *Inhabiting the Cruciform God: Kenosis, Justification, and Theosis in Paul's Narrative Soteriology* (Grand Rapids, Mich.: Eerdmans, 1982), p. 37.
10. This is an important corrective to perspectives that see humanity's ultimate future not as a promised land, a new heaven and new earth (Revelation 21), but as an other-worldly ethereal spiritual realm. See Anthony Hoekema, *The Bible and the Future* (Grand Rapids, Mich.: Eerdmans, 1994).
11. Webber, *Divine Embrace*, p. 175.